OCCASIONAL PA

Price Liberalization in Russia

Behavior of Prices, Household Incomes, and Consumption During the First Year

Vincent Koen and Steven Phillips

INTERNATIONAL MONETARY FUND
Washington DC
June 1993

Cataloging-in-Publication Data

Koen, Vincent.
Price liberalization in Russia : behavior of prices, household incomes, and consumption during the first year / Vincent Koen and Steven Phillips. — Washington, D.C. : International Monetary Fund, [1993]
p. ; cm. — (Occasional paper / International Monetary Fund, ISSN 0251-6365 ; 104)

ISBN 1-55775-295-8

1. Prices — Russia (Federation) 2. Income — Russia (Federation) 3. Consumption (Economics) — Russia (Federation) 4. Saving and investment — Russia (Federation) I. Phillips, Steven, 1961– II. Title III. Series: Occasional paper (International Monetary Fund) ; no. 104.
HD7035.2.K63 1993

Price: US$15.00
(US$12.00 to full-time faculty members and
students at universities and colleges)

Please send orders to:
International Monetary Fund, Publication Services
700 19th Street, N.W., Washington, D.C. 20431, U.S.A.
Tel.: (202) 623-7430 Telefax: (202) 623-7201

recycled paper

Contents

The following symbols have been used throughout this paper:

. . . to indicate that data are not available;

— to indicate that the figure is zero or less than half the final digit shown, or that the item does not exist;

– between years or months (e.g., 1991–92 or January–June) to indicate the years or months covered, including the beginning and ending years or months;

/ between years (e.g., 1991/92) to indicate a crop or fiscal (financial) year.

"Billion" means a thousand million.

Minor discrepancies between constituent figures and totals are due to rounding.

The term "country," as used in this paper, does not in all cases refer to a territorial entity that is a state as understood by international law and practice; the term also covers some territorial entities that are not states, but for which statistical data are maintained and provided internationally on a separate and independent basis.

Preface

Prices in Russia have been decontrolled in several steps since early 1991, after decades of near fixity. Their behavior before and after the January 1992 price liberalization is analyzed in this paper, as is the evolution of wages and overall consumer incomes and expenditures. Developments in 1992 are emphasized. Comparisons are made with recent experience in Central and Eastern Europe. Evidence on shortages, saving, and income distribution is also considered.

The authors are grateful to John Odling-Smee, Thomas Wolf, Benedicte Christensen, Michael Marrese, and Oleg Vjugin for comments on earlier drafts, Michel Le Marois and Robert Dippelsman for technical advice, the specialists of the State Statistical Committee of the Russian Federation and the Center of Economic Analysis and Forecasting for useful discussions, and Barbara Kaminska for research assistance. For information and insight on the reform experiences of Eastern Europe, thanks are due to Eric Clifton, Dimitrios Demekas, Luis Mendonca, Rolando Ossowski, and Tessa van der Willigen. Elin Knotter of the External Relations Department edited the manuscript and coordinated production of the publication.

The views expressed in the paper, as well as any errors, are the sole responsibility of the authors and should not be construed as those of the Russian authorities, Executive Directors of the IMF, or other members of the IMF staff.

I Introduction

Income and production developments in the Russian Federation began to diverge conspicuously in the late 1980s, when increases in the measured real wage significantly outstripped gains in measured productivity. After 1987, the growth of nominal wages and incomes accelerated, while the growth rate of output started to decline and finally turned negative. Under a regime of virtually fixed official prices, this divergence exacerbated shortages and led to a gradual loss of effective control over state-regulated prices. A gap emerged and widened between inflation in state stores and inflation in the control-free farmers' markets, one sign among others that major price adjustments were unavoidable. In early 1991, a first set of price reforms, combining discrete increases of controlled prices and the liberalization of other prices, was undertaken. By the end of 1991, however, the divergence from macroeconomic equilibrium had clearly worsened. As the convertibility of money into goods deteriorated rapidly, barter became widespread, particularly among enterprises. Effective January 2, 1992, a comprehensive price liberalization was implemented.

This paper documents and analyzes the behavior of prices, incomes, consumption, and savings before and after the January 1992 price liberalization, with emphasis on developments during 1992. The focus is on households more than on enterprises. Among the issues addressed are (1) What happened to consumer and producer prices when most were liberalized in January 1992; (2) why was their increase so large compared with the price liberalizations in Central and Eastern Europe of 1990–91; (3) to what extent did prices "overshoot"; (4) why has the rate of increase in producer prices outpaced that of consumer prices; (5) what evidence is there of a supply response and a decline in shortages as a result of price liberalization; (6) how did the real wage move before and after price liberalization; (7) what happened to household expenditures, saving, and real balances; and (8) what was the effect of price and income changes on the distribution of income and the standard of living?

Before addressing these questions, the limitations of the available statistics must be acknowledged. Virtually all the data used for Russia are produced by the State Statistical Committee of the Russian Federation (Goskomstat). It has gradually been modifying its statistical instruments to accord more closely with the needs of a market economy, frequently with the technical assistance of the statistical agencies of other countries and experts from international institutions. Nevertheless, many of the underlying methodological canons inherited from the days of central planning are still in place and appear increasingly ill suited as the economy becomes more market oriented. A further problem is the deterioration in reporting compliance, as the bureaucratic structure of the former centrally planned economy has broken down. Finally, some of the series available are shorter than required for analytical purposes: seasonal variations, for example, cannot be properly assessed. A number of more specific data problems are reported and discussed along the way.

Economic time series are difficult to interpret when major structural breaks occur. Therefore, cross-country comparisons are made in this study, showing how prices and wages moved in Russia, Poland, the former Czech and Slovak Federal Republic, Romania, and Bulgaria in the early stages of the transition to a market economy. While certain similarities are striking, the Russian experience in several respects appears extreme.

Section II discusses developments in producer and consumer prices and presents some evidence on shortages and the supply response to price liberalization. Section III traces the path of wages and other household incomes and depicts the apparent distributional impact of the early 1992 price burst. The response of household consumption and saving is the focus of Section IV, and a summary and some conclusions are provided in Section V. Tables appear in a statistical appendix.

II Prices and Shortages

Price reforms in Russia were carried out in several steps. Partial liberalization measures coupled with administrative price increases caused a sizable jump in producer prices in January 1991, and a comparably large burst in retail prices in April 1991. In the fall of 1991, the announcement of upcoming extensive liberalization measures and the gradual loss of central control over price setting resulted in accelerating open inflation. In early January 1992, as controls on most prices were officially lifted, and as remaining administered prices were raised several times over, a massive price jump was registered, both at the producer and retail levels. Additional liberalization measures followed, most notably in early March. After the price burst in January and throughout the summer, monthly inflation rates tended to decline, but remained very high, while shortages and queues for goods whose prices had been decontrolled shrank considerably. As a result of a significant loosening in financial policies, inflation increased in the fall of 1992.

Producer Prices

Decontrol Measures

An important reform of producer prices by the authorities of the former U.S.S.R. took place in January 1991, shifting many prices from the fixed to the "contractual" category.[1] After the reform, contractual prices accounted for 40 percent of the total in light industry, 50 percent in machine construction, and about 25 percent in the raw materials, energy, and metals sectors. As before the reform, the prices of "new products" were allowed to be set on a contract basis.[2]

As the dissolution of the former Soviet Union proceeded, the Government of the Russian Federation that took office in November 1991 prepared a bold program of price liberalization that had been announced in a presidential address on October 28, 1991. The corresponding decree was signed on December 3, 1991, and postponed the date of implementation from December 16 to January 2, 1992, on the request of other states of the former U.S.S.R.

The January 2, 1992 price liberalization resulted in about 80 percent of the producer prices being free (in value terms, at 1991 relative prices). A restricted list of producer goods and services remained controlled, including electricity and fuels, precious metals and stones, and freight tariffs.

The relative prices of energy products had long been very low by international standards. In January 1992, they were increased administratively about fivefold: the price for crude oil was raised to rub 350 a ton, the price of gas to rub 260 per thousand cubic meters, and the price of coal to rub 140 a ton (all excluding value-added tax—VAT). In the months following the January price jump, however, oil, gas, and coal producers were allowed to sell an increasing proportion of their output at free prices, amounting to 40 percent in early May in the oil and gas sectors, and equal to the output exceeding state orders in the coal sector.

A federal government decree on May 18 increased the administered price of oil and gas by four to six times, but at the same time abolished the right of producers to sell a proportion of their production at a price exceeding the administrative ceiling. Thus, the average effective price of oil and gas rose significantly less than the administered price.[3] The maximum price of oil was raised to rub 1,800–2,200 a ton (excluding VAT), with a steeply progressive tax applied on increments above rub 1,800. Similarly, the price of gas to industrial users was raised to rub 1,100–1,600 per thousand cubic meters (excluding VAT), with an analogous provision. Furthermore, in the second half of May, freight prices were liberalized.

Effective September 18, a federal government decree modified the tax schedule applicable to oil

[1] In theory, enterprises were permitted to negotiate "contract" prices for so-called new goods within administratively set limits. In practice, these prices reportedly were still heavily regulated and linked to state order prices.

[2] This reform also liberalized some retail prices.

[3] It was estimated that the average effective price for oil rose twofold to threefold rather than sixfold.

prices, introducing a tax of 30 percent on the price in excess of rub 4,000 a ton, 40 percent above rub 4,500 and 50 percent above rub 5,000, jointly with a 50 percent ceiling for the profitability ratio of oil producers. At the same time, coal prices were administratively raised by 30 percent.[4]

Methodology

The producer price index (PPI) published by Goskomstat covers industry and relies on fixed 1989 weights.[5] In contrast to what its denomination (*optoviy*) may suggest, this index measures prices at the factory gate rather than in wholesale trade. Hence, it excludes imported goods. The proliferation of barter deals, side payments, arrears, and discounts for cash, as well as reportedly widespread price discrimination,[6] suggests that PPI data should be interpreted with caution.

Developments

Industrial producer prices jumped, on average, fivefold in January 1992—after having more than tripled within 1991—with large interbranch variations (Table 1). Subsequently, these prices continued to grow rapidly, outpacing consumer prices by a large margin in February and March, and again from May to August (see Table 2 and Chart 1). Compared with the Central and East European experience, both the initial burst and the subsequent inflation were considerably larger in Russia (see Table 3 and Chart 2). Reasons for this outcome are discussed below.

One of the key categories of producer prices is that of energy carriers. During 1991, their relative level had fallen sharply: prices in the fuel industry, for example, had risen by 129 percent, in the petrochemical complex by 149 percent, and for electric energy by only 110 percent, while the overall industrial producer price index had increased by 236 percent. The relative domestic level of energy prices remained very low in the early months of 1992.[7] By end-June 1992—that is, after the second 1992 round of administered energy price increases—the average producer price of oil was still only about rub 1,900 a ton, which, evaluated at the interbank exchange rate, represented less than 9 percent of a prevailing world price of about $20 a barrel. Following the quasi-deregulation measures taken in September 1992, however, the producer price of oil almost tripled within a month, to about rub 5,700 a ton in October, or 12 percent of the world price ($19).[8] Gas and coal prices barely rose in the second half of 1992, implying a sharp decline both in dollar terms and in relative domestic terms. Overall, and even taking into account the possible undervaluation of the ruble by purchasing power parity standards, the price of energy remained very low in Russia in 1992.

Another important set of producer prices, not captured by the PPI, are agricultural procurement prices. The fragmentary evidence gathered on these prices suggests that they rose much less, and much later, than industrial prices. It also points to large distortions in relative prices, with grain reportedly purchased by the state at 70 percent and meat at only one-tenth of the world price as of September 1992 (Institute of Economic Policies, 1992).

Consumer Prices

Decontrol Measures

The April 1991 retail price reform undertaken by the authorities of the former U.S.S.R. reduced the share of fixed prices (to 55 percent), in favor of regulated prices (15 percent) and "contractual prices between the producer and the retail unit" (30 percent). In addition, certain fixed prices were raised to reduce relative price distortions and subsidies. Indeed, the reform at the producer level three months earlier had necessitated reform at the retail level, as the fiscal position was weakened by rising consumer price subsidies and falling turnover taxes.

As a result of the January 2, 1992 liberalization in

[4] The rules applicable to natural gas remained unchanged until end-January 1993, when its price was tripled.

[5] However, for reasons that remain unclear, cumulative price increases derived by chaining 12 successive monthly PPI inflation rates vastly exceed the corresponding month-over-12-month-earlier reported increases.

[6] See, for instance, *Rossiskaya Gazeta*, June 26 and 27, 1992, on the survey conducted by the Expert Appraisal Institute of the Russian Union of Industrialists and Entrepreneurs, suggesting that low prices are charged to "traditional customers," much higher prices (by 100–150 percent) are applied to "new partners," and even higher prices prevail on the commodity exchanges.

[7] In U.S. dollar terms, however, they rose substantially, owing to the sharp real appreciation of the ruble.

[8] This is the price reported by Goskomstat. An alternative benchmark would be the domestic price of oil reported by the Ministry of Fuel and Energy, which is the one paid by refineries and includes indirect taxes (except VAT) plus transport costs. This price had already reached rub 8,000 a ton in October 1992, or 16 percent of the world price (see Interfax, *Petroleum Report*, February 5–12, 1993). Moreover, the volatility of the real exchange rate should be taken into account when comparing ratios of domestic to world prices over time.

Chart 1. Inflation Rates
(Monthly percentage change)

Source: Goskomstat of the Russian Federation.
[1]Prior to January 1992, RPI for goods and services; thereafter, urban CPI.

Russia, about 90 percent of retail prices were in principle free (in value terms, at 1991 relative prices).[9] Price controls continued to apply to a number of basic consumer goods and services, including certain types of bread, milk and some milk products, baby foods, salt, sugar, vegetable oil, vodka and other spirits, electricity and fuels, matches, medicines, supplies for the disabled, housing rents, public utilities, and public transportation and communication services. Furthermore, the state distribution sector remained subject to a ceiling on its markup ratio, which was, however, raised to 25 percent (45 percent for the far northern regions). Administered prices for most of the above-mentioned goods were raised threefold to fivefold.

On March 7, 1992, a federal government decree allowed local authorities to abolish limits imposed on the prices of bread, milk, kefir, skim yogurt, sugar, salt, vegetable oil, and matches. This decision generalized the permission granted to local governments in January and February to adjust some of the regulated prices or to free them, as the budgetary resources required to maintain the controlled prices were not always forthcoming, causing some of the price ceilings to be exceeded.

Methodology

To interpret price movements in 1992, the methodology and meaning of the main price indices (presented in Table 2) should be clarified.[10]

The traditional retail price index (RPI) computed by Goskomstat is essentially a Paasche index. Weights are derived from information on current retail sales and paid services. Hence, the month-on-previous-month percentage changes of the RPI cannot be chained when the weights associated with the individual prices vary. In the early months of 1992, for example, the structure of consumption shifted rapidly, implying that chaining monthly RPI inflation data could distort actual price movements. The direction of the resulting net bias is ambiguous and depends on the relative strength of substitution and income effects. Lacking a monthly fixed-weight index, monthly RPI data have nevertheless been chained within 1991 to derive real wage levels (see Section III, below).[11] Other problems with the RPI relate to the fact that seasonal and other very short-term variations (such as strikes or unusual weather) influence the current weights,[12] and to the use of delivery as opposed to sales data in computing some of the weights (deliveries are typically more subject to "lumpiness" than sales). In addition, the collection of accurate retail turnover data becomes more

[9] This proportion would be much lower if calculated at free market prices rather than at 1991 prices. The overstatement of the degree of price liberalization inherent in such a figure may be considerable. For example, housing rents—which typically represent a large share of consumer expenditure in market economies—were controlled and would thus be given an artificially low weight in such a calculation.

[10] A more detailed discussion of the existing price indices is to be found in Koen and Phillips (1992).

[11] Chaining the monthly rates of change of the RPI for goods and services from December 1990 to December 1991 produces a cumulative price increase of 138 percent. This compares with a 144 percent rise in the corresponding fixed-weight CPI (see below), implying that in this case the distortion is not very large.

[12] A Laspeyres index would typically use weights relating to a full year.

Chart 2. Producer Price Inflation: International Comparison[1]
(Monthly percentage changes)

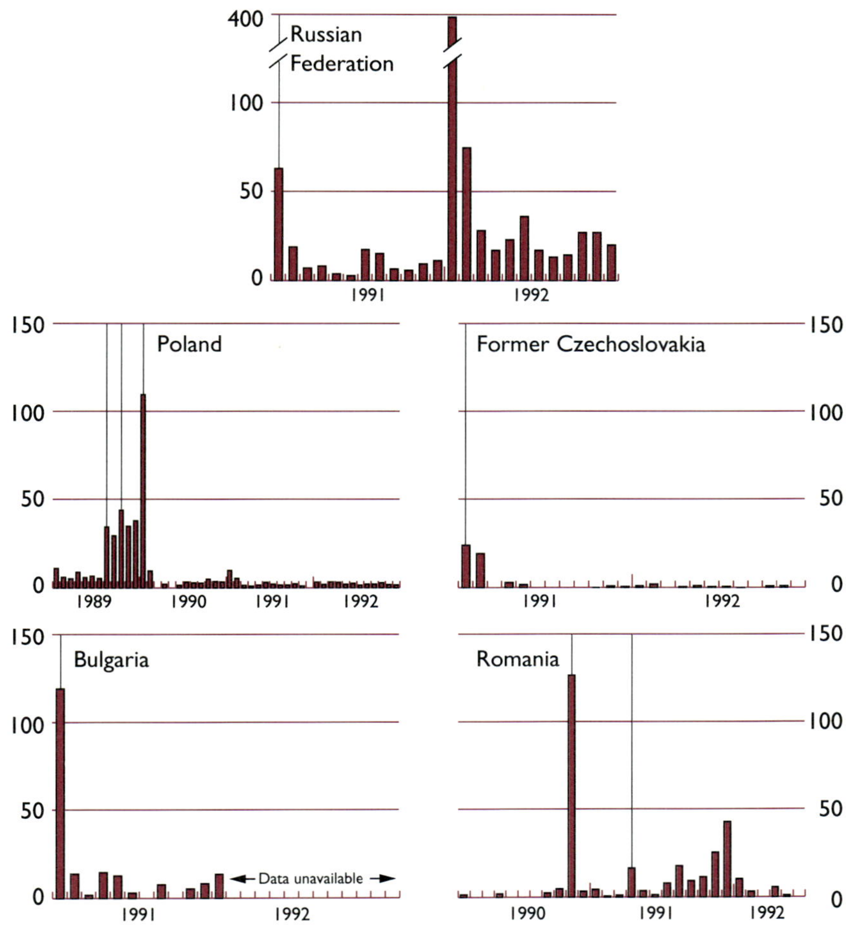

Sources: IMF, *International Financial Statistics*; OECD (1992); National Bank of Bulgaria, *Bank Review* (2/1992); and Goskomstat of the Russian Federation.

[1]Vertical lines denote months of significant price reform or liberalization.

difficult as distribution channels become more diversified.[13]

As an intermediate step en route to a standard Laspeyres consumer price index (CPI), Goskomstat introduced a "hybrid CPI." This index aggregates 140 subindices from the traditional RPI weighted by coefficients derived from a 1990 household budget survey, rather than from retail sales records. Since the hybrid CPI is a derivative of the RPI, however, it shares most of its weaknesses.

During the first half of 1992, a monthly Laspeyres CPI was developed, first for Moscow and then for an aggregation of 27 Russian urban areas. This nationwide index is henceforth referred to as the urban CPI. The reference group is workers' and employees' households (pensioners' and farm workers' households are excluded). The weights are fixed and reflect the structure of consumption of an average urban household in 1991–92 (the 1991 weights were adjusted to account for the change that

[13] But it could be argued that the use of current weights may be superior in cases in which the change in the composition of sales can be viewed as a disguised price change (for example, when the share of turnover on free markets rises relative to that of state stores for a good in increasingly short supply at the official price).

occurred in the first quarter of 1992).[14] The index is computed monthly from December 1991, but for comparison, the December 1990 value of the index has also been compiled. The underlying basket incorporates 262 items (compared with about 1,300 in the traditional RPI), with the main groups shown in Table 5. Each item is in principle priced at least at six outlets (including, when applicable, so-called street trading).

Other shortcomings of the indices used in this paper relate to the belated recognition of price increases that had been disguised as quality improvements, the aggregation problems encountered in the context of massive price liberalization, and the fact that the deflationary trends in black markets tend to be overlooked.[15] Finally, information on seasonality is insufficient to construct properly deseasonalized series.

Developments

Of particular interest are the size of the January 1992 price jump, the subsequent pattern of inflation, the extent of price reversion or overshooting, relative price changes, and the degree of price dispersion. Also important are some of the remaining restrictions to price setting and the ways in which price liberalization was in some cases less extensive de facto than de jure.

Price Jump of January 1992

The magnitude of the price jump in Russia in January 1992 (Chart 1) by far exceeded what had been observed in Central and Eastern Europe at the time of large-scale price liberalizations in 1990–91 (Chart 3). Depending on the index considered—and noting the predictably much smaller rise in the *kolkhoz* (collective farm) markets—prices increased, on average, threefold to fourfold in Russia in one month, whereas the largest monthly jump in the sample of the four Central and East European countries considered in Table 6 was a 123 percent increase (in Bulgaria). Several factors may explain why prices rose so much more in Russia.

One possible explanation is the effect on expectations of the Government's announcement in late 1991 that prices would rise by three to five times, and then the raising of certain key remaining administered prices by those amounts on January 2, 1992. Another indication of the size of the expected price jump was provided by the size of the nominal depreciation of the black market exchange rate between mid-October and end-December 1991. Assuming that the change in the exchange rate between the eve of the announcement and the eve of the actual price jump (correcting for intervening inflation) reflected the size of the anticipated adjustment in the price level, the expected price jump was only a little over two to two and a half times.

Another possible explanation is the existence of a larger monetary overhang in Russia than in other economies in transition. In relation to Poland, for example, where the extent of accumulated past repressed inflation in mid-1989 may have been similar in magnitude to that in Russia in late 1991, the significantly greater price burst in Russia following price liberalization could simply have reflected the fact that up to 50 percent of prices in Poland had already been liberalized before its stabilization program was initiated in January 1990.[16]

Finally, Russia's replacement of the traditional turnover tax and the recently instituted 5 percent sales tax by a 28 percent VAT in January 1992 may have played a role, but it would explain only a small fraction of the difference.

At the time of the price jump, numerous press reports mentioned price increases for individual items that were much larger than three to four times.[17] Table 7 and Chart 4 show that this was true locally for prices in state stores of various food items. Table 5 shows that the price of butter, on average, increased tenfold. Two factors were at work: on the one hand, as for butter, substantial relative price changes were needed to reduce previous distortions; on the other, price overshooting apparently did occur in a number of cases: Chart 4 shows significant reversion after January for beef prices, for example, and to a lesser extent for butter prices, in state stores in a number of cities. Similarly, Chart 5 reveals instances of overshooting for prices of beef, milk, and potatoes in some city markets. Even at the national level, the price of eggs overshot somewhat in January (Table 5). Weekly data show that nationwide overshooting was more widespread than monthly data may suggest, for ex-

[14] See Table 4. Within the food category, the consumption of bread products, potatoes, and eggs rose, while that of meat, dairy products, vegetables, and fruits declined.

[15] See Osband (1992) on these index number biases.

[16] In December 1991, money amounted to about three-fourths of annualized GDP in Russia. In Poland, the ratio of money to GDP had been about 90 percent in mid-1989, but partial price decontrols in subsequent months had reduced this ratio to one-third by the end of 1989. In January 1990, it continued to fall, to one-fourth. In Russia, this share dropped to one-fifth in January 1992. For further discussion of the experience in Central and Eastern Europe, see Bruno (1992) and the sources cited therein.

[17] This may represent a selection bias, as examples of above-average price rises may be deemed more newsworthy than examples of smaller price increases.

Chart 3. Consumer Price Inflation: International Comparison[1]
(Monthly percentage changes)

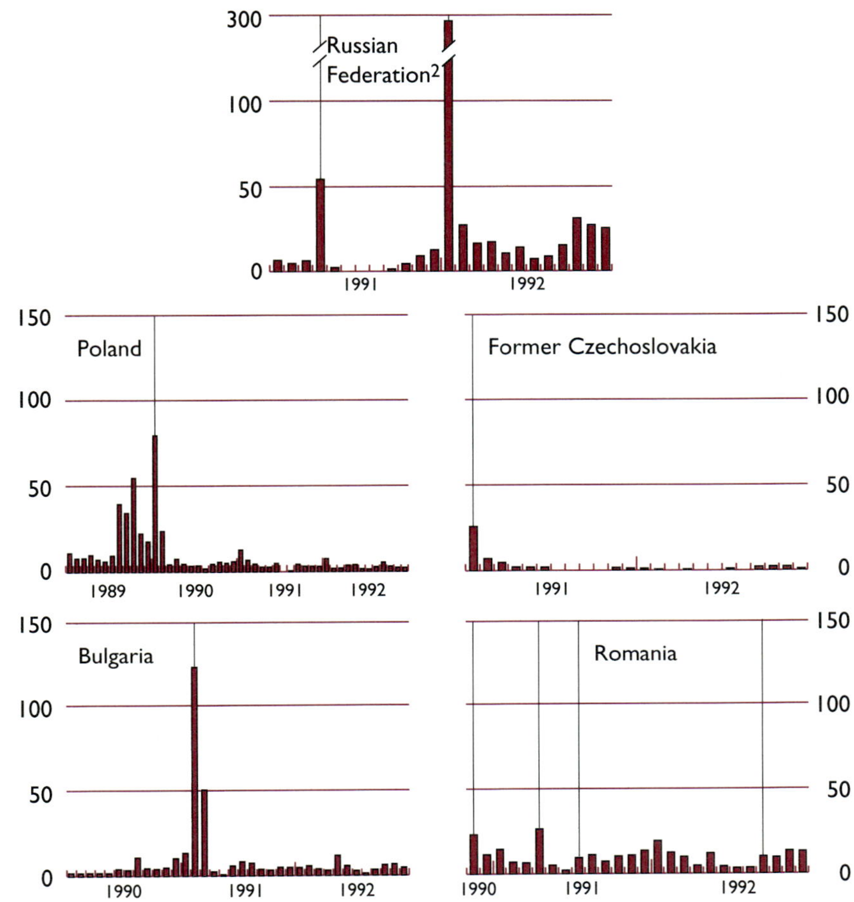

Sources: IMF, *International Financial Statistics*; Bulgarian National Bank; and Goskomstat of the Russian Federation.
[1]Vertical lines denote months of significant price reform or liberalization.
[2]Prior to January 1992, RPI for goods and services; thereafter, urban CPI.

ample, for beef and vegetable oil.[18] Whether the overall consumer price level overshot is a more difficult issue, discussed in Section IV.

[18] A more accurate assessment of the degree of overshooting requires information on seasonality. Price reversion is also a priori more likely for perishable goods (although it appears that large quantities of meat, for example, remained unsold). Finally, a control should be included for the reduction of the VAT rate from 28 percent to 15 percent for a number of basic foodstuffs in early 1992.

Subsequent Inflation

Inflation following the price jump was also relatively high in Russia, remaining in the double digits throughout the first half of 1992, whereas it subsided to single-digit levels within two months in most of Central and Eastern Europe (Table 6). In July and August 1992, the rate of monthly consumer price inflation finally dropped below 10 percent, in part reflecting the seasonality of some food prices. In each of the next two months, however, it dou-

Chart 4. Food Prices in State Stores Across Cities,[1] December 1991–December 1992
(In rubles per kilogram or liter)

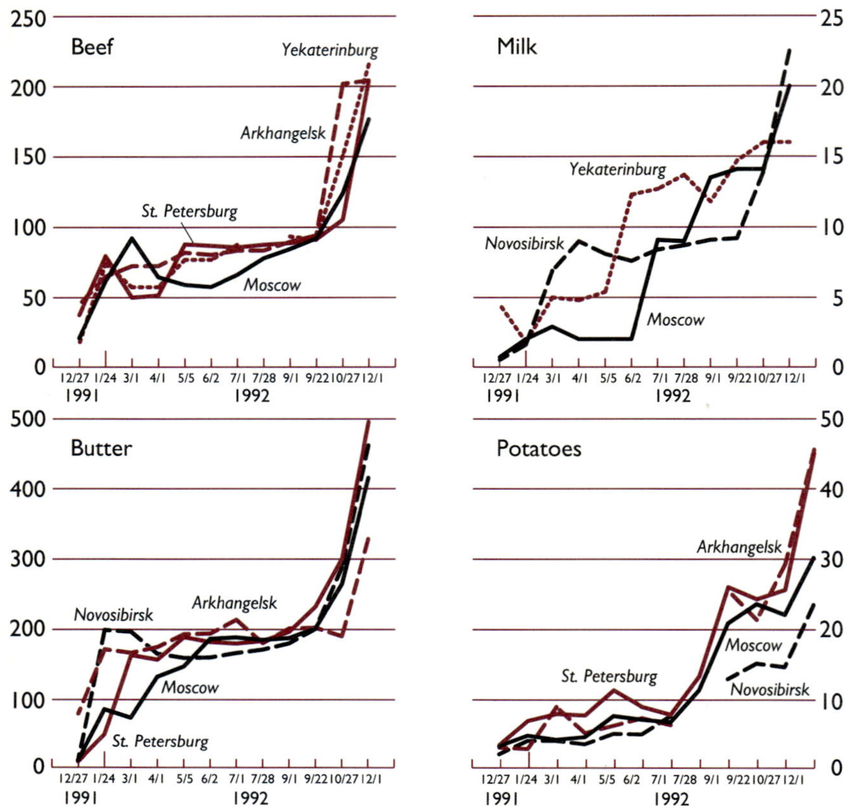

Sources: Goskomstat of the Russian Federation; and Interfax, *Agriculture Report*.
[1]When only a range of prices was available, the midpoint was used.

bled, to 15 percent in September and 31 percent in October. In November and December 1992 and into the early months of 1993, consumer price inflation remained above 20 percent. The acceleration of inflation resulted mainly from a loosening of financial policies in the third quarter of 1992.[19]

Relative Prices

One of the key relative prices is that of food, which changed significantly in both 1991 and 1992. During 1991, the relative price of food rose by about 12 percent compared with overall consumer prices (as measured by the urban CPI); in January 1992, it jumped by a further 16 percent. It fell somewhat during the next few months, but rose again from June onward, and ended the year 25 percent above its December 1990 base.[20] Given the large weight of food items in the urban CPI, it can be seen that the increase in their price relative to the nonfood component of the CPI was much larger: 65 percent in the two years ended December 1992. In part, these developments are related to the removal (and rein-

[19] See International Monetary Fund (1993) for a discussion of policies.

[20] These results are not independent of the index used. For instance, if relative price developments are measured with the hybrid CPI, the within-1992 pattern is similar, but the end-1992 level is 15 percent below the December 1990 base.

Chart 5. Food Prices in City Markets Across Cities,[1] December 1991–December 1992
(In rubles per kilogram or liter)

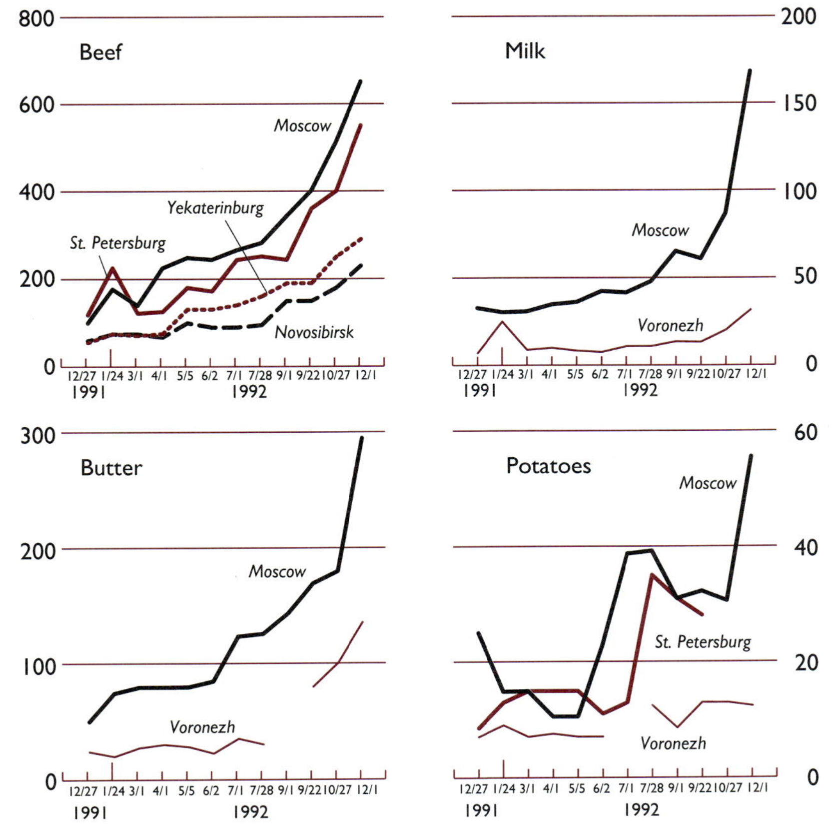

Sources: Goskomstat of the Russian Federation; and Interfax, *Agriculture Report*.
[1]When only a range of prices was available, the midpoint was used.

troduction, in some cases) of food price subsidies. They probably also reflect shifts in relative supply and demand of food versus nonfood items.

The relative price of services declined sharply during 1991 and dropped further in January 1992. From February 1992 through midyear, it recovered somewhat, but remained low compared with its historical level. In the second half of 1992, it declined again for such groups as rents and utilities but rose substantially for transport and communications.

Another key relative price is that of energy. During 1991, the consumer prices of gasoline, electricity, and natural gas barely rose, and consequently fell sharply in relative terms. In 1992, gasoline prices increased by more than 70 times, implying that their domestic relative level more than tripled compared with December 1991 (but rose by only about a third compared with December 1990). In contrast, the price of electricity increased by only 9 times between December 1991 and December 1992, and its relative domestic price plummeted by more than 60 percent compared with end-1991, and by 85 percent compared with end-1990.

In U.S. dollar terms, the price of gasoline (evaluated at the interbank exchange rate) amounted to about one-sixth of the U.S. or one-twentieth of the German price by mid-1992, and to about one-fifth of the U.S. or one-fifteenth of the German price at the end of 1992. The price of electricity for households was about 1.5 percent of that in the United States and 0.8 percent of the German price by mid-1992, and dropped further, to 0.8 percent of the

U.S. and 0.4 percent of the German price in the second half of 1992.[21]

Price Dispersion

Although a certain degree of geographical price dispersion is to be expected in any country, in Russia the geographical price dispersion registered around the time of the price jump, and for some items in the following months as well, seems extreme. In part, this dispersion probably reflects the fact that distances are great, implying higher transportation costs and greater potential for local monopoly power. Also, local subsidization varies considerably, as can be inferred from the much smaller geographical price dispersion across city markets (or "free markets") than that across state stores.

That prices sometimes varied by a factor of ten or more in state stores (Table 7) may also reflect the price uncertainty and confusion that is bound to accompany radical liberalization. The large price differences observed even within cities for some items corroborate this conjecture. This effect should be largely dissipated after a few months, however, and indeed for a number of goods, geographical dispersion dropped remarkably between end-December 1991 and July–August 1992, presumably because of declining subsidies, increasing competition, and diminishing price uncertainty. For example, the coefficients of variation for prices in state stores fell sharply between end-December 1991 and end-July 1992 for beef, eggs, milk, butter, and vegetable oil.[22] In the last months of 1992, however, price dispersion tended to rise anew for beef, eggs, milk, and butter, possibly as a result of increasingly divergent local price policies in a context of accelerating inflation.[23] The same evolution for the dispersion measure was observed for milk, for a broader sample of 75 cities.[24]

Another dimension of price dispersion is the discrepancy between prices in city markets and prices in state stores (Table 8). In 1991, prices in *kolkhoz* markets were on average almost six times as high as those in state trade. In early 1992, this ratio fell dramatically, but varied considerably across products and regions. For milk, for instance, they remained significantly above unity throughout 1992, as milk sales in state stores generally continued to be subsidized. For eggs, butter, or potatoes, by contrast, they fell rapidly, even dropping below unity in some cases. As for regional variations, the Moscow price ratios were typically among the highest throughout 1992.

The regional variations in inflation rates are also noteworthy. For selected individual food items, these differences can be derived from the data presented in Table 7. At the aggregate level, a comparison of the last two columns of Table 2 shows that consumer prices rose more rapidly in 1991 in Moscow than in the rest of the country; accordingly, the January 1992 price jump was smaller in the capital.

Remaining Restrictions to Price Setting

Price liberalization was in some cases short-lived: for example, it was reported around mid-March 1992 that the Krasnoyarsk *krai* had reverted to price controls and subsidies on bread and milk after one week of free prices. Table 9 shows the extent of remaining controls on food prices in mid-1992.

Another limitation on the freedom to set prices was the obligation for enterprises classified as monopolists by the state anti-monopoly committee to notify the State Committee on Prices (Goskomtsen) of increases in their prices and to abide by predefined limits (varying across branches) on profitability ratios.[25] It remained unclear, however, to what extent these rules could be enforced in practice.[26]

An indirect way to limit food price increases has been for *oblasts* (provinces) that are surplus producers of agricultural products (particularly meat and dairy products) to ban exports to other *oblasts*. By mid-1992, such trade barriers had reportedly been erected in 23 areas.[27] Similar restrictions have

[21] The U.S. and German prices used are those published in International Energy Agency (1993). For the price of electricity in Russia, an unweighted average of the (higher) price charged in urban areas and the (lower) price charged in rural areas was used.

[22] Respectively, from 0.41 to 0.12, from 0.31 to 0.11, from 0.96 to 0.32, from 0.97 to 0.07, and from 1.26 to 0.28. A notable exception is potatoes, for which the coefficient of variation rose from 0.19 to 0.27 during the first half of 1992.

[23] The associated coefficients of variation increased respectively to 0.15, 0.23, 0.38, and 0.38 by early December 1992.

[24] See International Monetary Fund (1993).

[25] This regulation applied to both producer and consumer prices, although it included various exemptions. This form of regulation was somewhat weakened by being essentially of an ex post nature; nevertheless, it did restrict the ability of sellers to set prices freely and presumably reduced the incentive to minimize costs.

[26] On December 31, 1992, the Prime Minister signed an ordinance that tightened and extended the scope of the price restrictions applicable so far only to monopolists. It was revoked, however, on January 18, 1993.

[27] See Institute of Economic Policies (1992). In December 1992, the Mayor of Moscow restricted shipments of champagne, alcohol, or sweets out of the city by local producers (*Nezavisimaya Gazeta*, December 17, 1992).

reportedly been imposed on industrial goods. Local authorities in a number of areas have also been reported to require local producers to sell a portion of their output at below-market prices and to have used the goods so acquired in interregional barter. Among the levers at the disposal of the local authorities in these instances was their control over the distribution of licenses and over access by producers to subsidies and inputs.

Divergence Between Producer and Consumer Prices

Just as the industrial PPI had risen much faster than consumer prices in 1991, it continued to do so during the first half of 1992. As a result, the cumulative wedge between these two indicators had become enormous by mid-1992. Taking December 1990 as a base of 100, the urban CPI had risen to 2,113, whereas the industrial PPI had grown to 7,106, that is, almost three and a half times more.[28] This divergence cannot be explained by the lag usually observed between changes in producer and consumer prices, since the divergence increased almost monotonically. For the same reason, it cannot be accounted for by one-time factors such as that in January 1992 shops were obliged to sell existing inventories at no more than twice (for food products) or three times (for other products) their December 1991 prices. The definition of the PPI, the differential coverage of the indices under consideration, the role of price controls and subsidies, and the financial counterpart of higher producer prices may better explain the divergence.

The PPI may reflect listed prices rather than prices actually charged. It may not reflect the significant discounts that were reportedly available for cash payment, particularly during the period of the so-called cash shortage in the first half of 1992. Also, the PPI encompasses exports to other states of the former Soviet Union, which for some products were made at prices higher than domestic prices. Another factor may be the large amount of consumer price subsidies pledged and paid out following some of the producer price increases, in particular those for energy carriers. For example, the mid-May increase in oil and gas prices at the producer level was followed by increases in subsidies for passenger transportation and for fuel used by the population. However, sizable producer subsidies were also granted to some primary energy consuming sectors, in particular the electric power generation, chemical, cement, and paper industries, as well as to some consumers of secondary energy (electric power and petrochemicals), notably agriculture.[29] Hence, the net impact of subsidization on the wedge between producer and retail prices is ambiguous.[30]

Finally, the exponential growth of enterprise arrears during the first half of 1992 undoubtedly played an important role. Total arrears rose from rub 34 billion on January 1 to rub 666 billion on April 1 and to rub 3.2 trillion on July 1.[31] One implication was that recorded producer prices were contract prices but not necessarily settlement prices. It is likely that once payments arrears became common practice, sellers started to augment their quoted prices by the expected present value of the implied inflation tax. In Romania, where interenterprise arrears also exploded, industrial producer prices also rose much faster than consumer prices. In Bulgaria and the former Czechoslovakia, by contrast, where interenterprise arrears remained much smaller, no such discrepancy arose. In Poland, where interenterprise arrears grew much less than in Russia following the January 1990 price liberalization, consumer prices rose somewhat faster than producer prices. The "hardness" of the budget constraints faced by Russian enterprises was dubious; by contrast, households were liquidity constrained (literally, by a cash shortage, as well as by the absence of consumer credit). Thus the growth of prices of consumer goods was probably relatively more limited by demand than that of the intermediate and capital goods sold to other enterprises, whose exclusion from the CPI may help account for its much smaller increase than the PPI in 1992.

That prices in the "food industry" component of the PPI rose by much less than those of the industrial goods in the PPI in the first six months of 1992 supports this interpretation. Indeed, the increase of 995 percent was not much greater than the increase

[28] The second number is derived by chaining the monthly 1992 inflation rates with the increase from December 1990 to December 1991.

[29] This suggests that the effective increase in the relative price of energy may have been smaller than suggested by the movements in intersectoral terms of trade discussed earlier.

[30] The large amounts and multiple guises of subsidization in the Russian economy in 1992 are discussed in International Monetary Fund (1993).

[31] Of the stock of rub 3.2 trillion on July 1, rub 2.3 trillion represented interenterprise arrears for deliveries of goods and services (excluding arrears vis-à-vis enterprises in other states of the former Soviet Union) and rub 0.9 trillion, arrears to the budget and on other obligations. Only partial information on the stock of arrears is available beyond July 1, but its growth probably slowed considerably thereafter, when credit expansion accelerated and the process of netting out the July 1 stock of arrears began (see International Monetary Fund, 1993).

of 820 percent in the food, beverages, and tobacco component of the CPI.[32]

The convergence of producer and consumer price inflation rates in the second half of 1992, following the introduction in July of a prepayment rule among enterprises and coinciding with the relaxation of financial policies and the likely slowdown in the accumulation of new arrears, points in the same direction.

Shortages

One of the main objectives of price liberalization was to increase the price level relative to money holdings and to reduce relative price distortions and thereby eliminate shortages and queues. At the retail level, direct evidence on the latter can be found in crude statistics on the availability of selected items in state stores. Other, indirect evidence includes the path of prices on free markets and in state stores for specific goods and the level of inventories in the distribution sector. The diversification of sales outlets is another indicator. At the producer level, some evidence of a supply response is perceptible as well but cannot be readily isolated in the chaotic context of 1992.

A rudimentary measure of shortages is the proportion of cities where selected goods are deemed available in state stores (Table 10). By that token, food shortages shrank considerably during the first quarter of 1992. This measure is discontinuous, however, in two respects: cities are not weighted by their population or by some other relevant criterion; and the variable under consideration is a discrete one. Hence, percentages should not be interpreted too literally. In addition, shortages remained acute for some products, such as sugar or vegetable oil, for which waves of panic buying continued to be reported intermittently through the end of 1992.

Other indicators also suggest a decline in shortages. The ratio of free market prices to prices in state stores fell sharply for many products across cities (Table 8). For a number of products, they came down to unity (or, exceptionally, even slightly below).

Chart 6. Inventories in Retail Trade
(In turnover days)

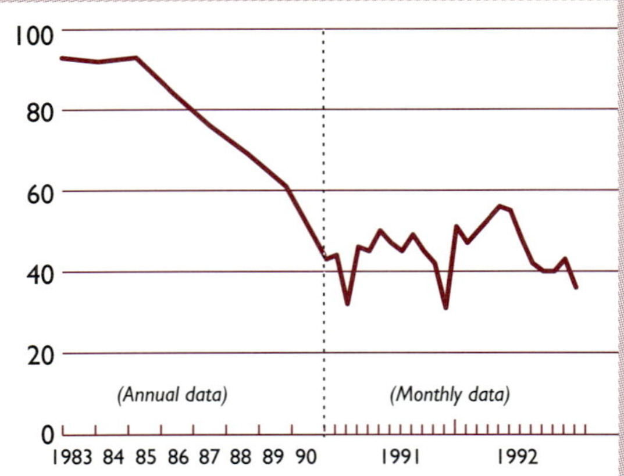

Source: Goskomstat of the Russian Federation.

Inventories in retail trade also rose substantially in the early months of 1992, even if they remained low by historical standards (Chart 6). The interpretation of available inventory statistics, however, is far from straightforward. The valuation rules determining the ruble amount of inventories are unclear. Moreover, because inventories simultaneously reflect demand and supply factors, their recent recovery cannot be viewed purely as a positive supply response.[33]

Another striking development has been the surge of street trading, legalized by a January 1992 presidential decree, similar to what had been observed in Central and Eastern Europe. In part, street trading is carried out by producers bypassing the traditional distribution channels. However, a significant proportion of the items on display are reportedly resold in the streets by individuals who have acquired them in state stores (although possibly through the back door). Street trading in that situation can be a sign that shortages in state stores have not completely vanished.

At the producer level, the output mix changed in reaction to the relative price shifts. For example, in the dairy sector, the large increase in the relative retail price of butter was accompanied by a sharp output shift from milk to butter, with production of

[32] This points to a sharp deterioration of the intersectoral terms of trade faced by the so-called agroindustrial complex since 1991. Substantial anecdotal evidence suggests such a shift (although if all the press reports on the relative prices of inputs and outputs across sectors were accepted, it would have to be concluded that virtually all faced a dramatic squeeze; while this conclusion seems unlikely, it is not impossible in principle, depending on how adverse the developments in foreign trade prices actually were). The impact on net incomes across sectors also depends, however, on the distribution of taxes and subsidies, which presumably partly offset the impact of the intersectoral price divergence.

[33] Also relevant would be the behavior of stocks held by consumers. On this point, see Weitzman (1991).

milk falling by 29 percent during the first quarter of 1992 (compared with the same period a year earlier), while output of butter rose by 8 percent.[34] A more comprehensive analysis of the supply response would have to control for shortages (excess demand), for differential consumer and producer subsidies as well as for exogenous disruptions in interenterprise links (and also, of course, for the decline in aggregate consumer demand).[35]

[34] The price of butter relative to that of milk increased fourfold between December 1990 and the first quarter of 1992 (Table 5).

[35] Further information on the change in the composition of output in 1992 is provided in International Monetary Fund (1993).

III Household Incomes

An important phenomenon of the late 1980s was the growth of nominal incomes and wages considerably in excess of price increases or any conceivable advances in labor productivity. The ensuing growing macroeconomic disequilibrium was reflected in worsening shortages and the accumulation of undesired holdings of financial wealth. By the end of 1991, the divergence of nominal incomes and prices was extreme.

This continued and accelerating buildup of excess real wages and a presumptive monetary overhang set the stage for the large jump in the price level when prices were liberalized. On the eve of the January 2, 1992 price liberalization, the size of this jump was not the only uncertainty; the behavior of wages was also in question. Would a sustained correction in the real wage follow, in contrast to the aftermath of the 1991 price reforms? If so, how would the new real wage compare with historical levels? Would the price burst trigger a wage-price spiral that the monetary authorities might feel compelled to validate? These questions, as well as the intersectoral and overall distribution of income and poverty are considered in this section. Real wage developments in Russia are also compared with the recent experience of other economies that have undergone comprehensive liberalizations.

Wages and Other Incomes

Methodology

Two main types of evidence are available from Goskomstat for the study of income developments: average wages and the so-called money incomes of the population—a measure of household income. The average wage data have their origin in the total wage fund figures reported by enterprises to Goskomstat. This series, which traditionally was compiled only annually, became available quarterly, and then monthly, in 1991. In addition to an overall national average, average wages in various sectors of the economy are published.

The household incomes data represent a broader concept, including, for example, pension payments, stipends, family allowances, and interest income. These data are available annually as part of the Goskomstat table, "Money Incomes and Expenditures of the Population," which also permits calculation of the saving rate of households. Household income on an annual frequency is computed by aggregating direct estimates of the various types of incomes. On a monthly frequency, however, the published money income figures are the sum of estimates of household saving and of expenditure. Although the monthly incomes data are of considerable interest for analyzing events in 1992, their reliability is much less certain, as discussed below. Also, in recent years the monthly data have at times been strongly influenced by special lump-sum "compensation" payments to households' deposits (for example, in April and July 1991, and in April 1992—see Table 11, footnote 2). Statistics on income distribution (and on the structure of consumer expenditures) are based on a monthly household budget survey conducted by Goskomstat on a sample of almost 50,000 units.

The Goskomstat wage and household incomes data differ significantly in how they were influenced by the so-called cash shortage that became very acute in the first half of 1992, when numerous reports indicated that many workers were receiving less income than promised by their employers. Almost all Russian workers (except the military) are used to being paid in cash, twice a month. However, because of the cash shortage, some enterprises were unable to obtain from the banking system the currency needed to make all wage payments. This situation led, in some cases, to the relatively new phenomenon of enterprises making transfers to the savings bank accounts of employees as a substitute means of payment. A worker receiving such a transfer, however, may also have been unable to convert it into cash.[36] Of course, the failure of some enter-

[36] Cash has traditionally been the almost exclusive means of payment for households in Russia. Therefore, these aspects of the cash shortage may have been important in restricting the demand for consumer goods.

prises to make promised wage payments was attributable not to the cash shortage but rather to their own financial difficulties.

Goskomstat wage data reflect wages earned, rather than wage payments actually received, during a given period. As discussed below, the difference between these concepts was significant in the first half of 1992. In contrast, the money incomes data in principle correspond to payments actually received, but are probably subject to greater measurement error.

In analyzing incomes data, the focus here is their rate of growth relative to that of prices. The implied statistical or measured real wage is to be distinguished, especially prior to 1992, from the real wage concept used in studying market economies, and which can be considered an indicator of consumer welfare if wages and incomes in the form of money are freely convertible into goods at market-clearing prices. This was not so in the "shortage economy" that prevailed in Russia before January 1992.[37] Indeed, the statistical real wage measured before that date is of interest more as an indicator of macroeconomic disequilibrium than as an indicator of consumer welfare.

Finally, in constructing a real wage series with a base year of 1987, Goskomstat's retail price index (RPI) is used through 1991; beginning in 1992, the urban CPI is used. Although the RPI is imperfect (as discussed in Section II), the limited flexibility of the price level during most of the period prior to 1992 implies that variation owing to error in measuring the price level is likely to be small in relation to the magnitude of wage inflation. Thus, the main findings of this section are probably robust to the price level mismeasurement occurring before the 1992 price liberalization.

Developments

The growth of average wages began to outpace significantly the growth of retail prices in 1988, resulting in a steady increase of the statistical real wage (Chart 7). By 1990, average real wages stood 27 percent above their 1987 levels. The price reforms of early 1991 abruptly canceled this buildup, lowering the national average and industrial real wages approximately to their 1987 levels in the second quarter. However, although retail prices were quite stable for some time after the April 1991 price reform, wage inflation continued: the national average wage rose 30 percent in the third quarter of 1991, reversing the recent real adjustment. In the final quarter of the year, retail price inflation accelerated to 16 percent, but was again outpaced by a 64 percent surge in the average wage (73 percent in industry). By December 1991, statistical real wages were more than twice their 1987 levels.[38]

In early 1992, nominal wage growth continued, with the national average wage rising 20 percent in January (41 percent in industry).[39] The statistical real wage, however, fell precipitously with the January price burst, by roughly two-thirds. As Chart 7 makes clear, a large part of this decline represented a reversal of increases experienced only in late

Chart 7. Nominal and Real Average Wages[1]

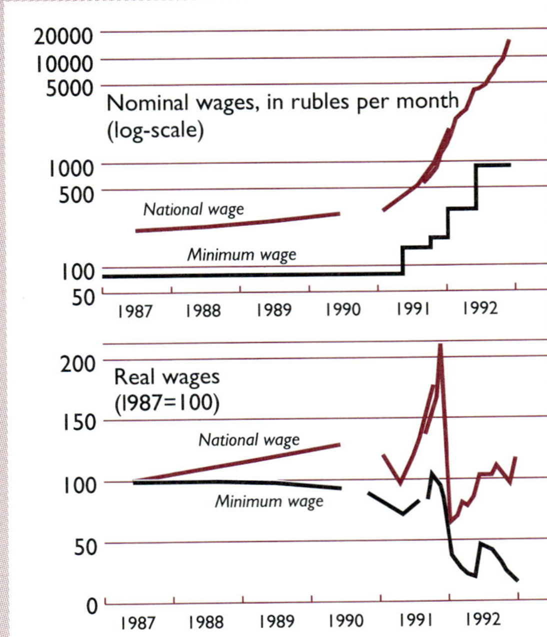

Sources: Goskomstat of the Russian Federation; and authors' estimates.

[1]Annual data for 1987–90, quarterly for 1991, monthly for September 1991–December 1992; not adjusted for arrears on wage payments.

[37] As discussed above, although shortages were still observed in Russia in 1992, they may be considered more microeconomic in nature, at least in contrast to the situation before January 1992, which clearly was one of excess aggregate supply of financial assets and excess aggregate demand for goods.

[38] This extreme outcome can be only partially explained by the seasonal bonus payments to wage earners in December.

[39] A point sometimes overlooked is that if an accumulated monetary overhang is sufficiently large, its elimination may require a jump not only in the price level but also in the average wage. Only by coincidence would the price level jump required to eliminate the monetary overhang also reduce the real wage by exactly the required amount.

1991, and only in a context of widespread shortages and an unsustainable rundown of retail inventories. Nevertheless, statistical real wages dropped below 1987 levels. Furthermore, in contrast to the experience after the (largely administered) price increases of early 1991, the January 1992 decline in the statistical real wage was not completely reversed. The real wage did grow strongly, however, after the January price burst, with overall real wages rising at an average monthly rate of 10 percent from January through June. By June 1992 the relationship between the national average wage and consumer prices was approximately the same as in 1987; a broadly similar real wage level was subsequently maintained through the end of 1992.

This evidence appears to contradict numerous reports that as a result of price liberalization in early 1992 the standard of living of most Russian citizens had fallen to levels not seen in recent memory. In this connection, several points addressed later may be especially relevant: first, the average level of income may conceal significant developments at the lower end of the income distribution; second, income after taxes—including the inflation tax—might not have moved in tandem with average wages. A third factor concerns wage and other arrears.

Wage Arrears

Actual wage payments were less than indicated by the wage data analyzed here, which do not reflect wage arrears. Monthly information on the latter is available from April 1, 1992 onward (Table 12).[40] The stock of arrears grew rapidly in the second quarter of 1992, and peaked toward the middle of the year. Its growth was mainly associated with the increasingly acute shortage of cash. The volume of arrears outstanding fell swiftly as credit expansion accelerated and notes of larger denomination were introduced in the summer. In industry, the total stock of wage arrears in real terms (using consumer prices as a deflator) had declined to about one-fifth of its peak level by the last quarter of 1992 (Chart 8). The remaining arrears were attributable to the financial distress of enterprises rather than to the cash shortage. The share of the industrial sector in the wage arrears recorded in industry, agriculture, and construction peaked in mid-1992, and declined thereafter. By end-1992, wage arrears were still recorded in every sixth industrial firm and in every fifth enterprise in construction and agriculture.

The implications of wage arrears for the level of actual wage payments, as opposed to wages accrued, can be tentatively quantified for industry. In the second quarter of 1992, only 86 percent of the wages due were paid out in this sector, with a trough in May (75 percent). The inflation tax borne by wage earners on these arrears in the second quarter amounted to about 3 percent of the wage bill.[41]

Chart 8. Wage Arrears in Industry,[1] April–December 1992
(In percent of wage bill in month ended)

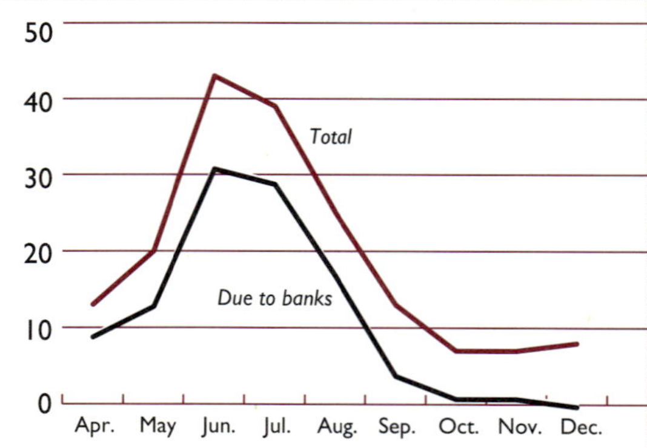

[1]Stock outstanding at the beginning of the month.

Sustainable Wage Level

Although the appropriate level of the real wage in Russia is difficult to determine, the following observations may be made. There is some disagreement in the literature on whether substantial macroeconomic disequilibrium (in the form of a monetary overhang and excess real wages) had been long standing or whether it had developed only in the late 1980s.[42] If the latter is true, the 1987 base year considered here seems a reasonable benchmark, given the strong divergence of measured wage and price growth that began in 1988. Supposing that in 1987 the real wage per unit of aggregate output was approximately appropriate, subsequent real wage developments may be considered in conjunction

[40] Arrears on wages, pensions, and other payments to households were already reported as a serious problem in late 1991.

[41] This is an ex post measure, ignoring the costs associated with uncertainty about wage payments. It is also an aggregate measure, abstracting from likely significant variation across enterprises. Finally, it does not reflect the costs implied by binding liquidity constraints.

[42] One piece of evidence in support of the former view is that according to Goskomstat prices of agricultural products in *kolkhoz* markets were almost two and a half times as high as those in state stores already in the mid-1980s.

with developments in both aggregate output and employment.

Clearly, the rise of the measured real wage from 1987 through December 1991 was far in excess of any conceivable improvement in aggregate labor productivity. In fact, rough calculations of productivity suggest a substantial cumulative decline (reflecting mostly the abrupt fall in output that began in 1990–91). The drop in the real wage that occurred in January 1992 appears to have more than offset this decline. However, the recovery of the real wage to its 1987 level, by June 1992, together with the further decline in 1992 of all indicators of aggregate output, suggests that by mid-1992 the real wage per unit of output was again significantly above its benchmark 1987 level. Since output continued to decline in the second half of 1992, and since the real wage on average remained above its 1987 base, the same conclusion holds a fortiori for the end of 1992.

One important caveat with respect to the norm defined in this way is that an increase in labor's share of national income during the regime switch is not necessarily inappropriate. The decline in the role of public consumption (most notably military procurement) may make room for additional private consumption. Similarly, the traditionally high share of investment and particularly of stockbuilding in national output may be considered a reflection of the inefficiencies of central planning. If these inefficiencies can be reduced, a given level of aggregate output will be consistent with a greater share for labor income and private consumption. Therefore, the sustainable level of wages may be higher than the apparent productivity-adjusted 1987 benchmark.

Comparison with Other Transition Economies

Chart 9 depicts real wage developments, since 1987, in four transition economies as well as Russia. It is not meant to imply that real wages in 1987 represented equilibrium values in any or all of these economies, but simply to allow a basic comparison of real wage developments during the transition. For example, in Bulgaria and Romania, the increase in real wages prior to general liberalization of prices was much smaller than in Russia; in the former Czechoslovakia, almost no divergence of wages and prices had occurred. In each of these three cases, however, real wages fell steeply in early 1991 following price liberalization.

The Russian experience appears to be closer to that of Poland, particularly with respect to the much larger growth of the statistical real wage prior to general price liberalization. In Poland, however, the decline from the peak real wage value was less abrupt, as it began with the partial liberalization of prices in August 1989. At its lowest point just after the comprehensive January 1990 liberalization, the Polish real wage was about three-fourths of its 1987 level; the corresponding low point for real wages in Russia was fairly similar, at about 75 percent in industry and 65 percent overall. In Russia as well as in Poland, the former Czechoslovakia, and Bulgaria, real wages recovered significantly within the six months following general price liberalization, after which they remained relatively stable. Only in Russia, however, did the average wage recover to beyond its real 1987 level, whereas the cumulative output drop was at least as severe in Russia as in any of the comparator countries.

Wage developments can also be compared across countries by computing wages in terms of U.S. dollars (Chart 10). In January 1992, the average wage in Russia, valued at the interbank exchange rate, was only $7 a month, compared with $65 in Poland in January 1990. A strong real appreciation then followed, but the average Russian wage peaked in June 1992 at only about $40 a month, and fluctuated in the second half of 1992 between $25 and $40. In contrast, the average dollar wage rose steadily in Poland to $100 by mid-1990 and to $160 by end-1990. In Bulgaria, dollar wages more than doubled after declining abruptly at the time of price liberalization, to about $60 one year later. In the former Czechoslovakia, dollar wages also increased substantially at the same stage of the transition, to about $160 in late 1991. In Romania (where the temporary persistence of a system of multiple exchange rates complicates the analysis), dollar wages evolved in a more convoluted fashion, but hovered at about $50 one year after price liberalization. In all comparator countries except Romania, the apparent trend increase in the dollar wage characterizing the first year of the transition continued in the next year. Such comparisons (or comparisons with wage levels in countries outside Central and Eastern Europe) do not, however, control for differences with respect to nonwage entitlements benefiting workers, which are particularly important in Russia (housing privileges, subsidized food, child care, vacations, etc).[43] Moreover, the exchange rates used in such comparisons may not be strictly comparable over time and across countries, and deviations from purchasing power parity presumably also vary considerably within the sample. Also, the wage data used here are not deseasonalized.

Incomes Policy

Incomes policy was considered an important component of the stabilization programs of the Central

[43] These nonwage benefits declined less than wages in 1992 in Russia.

Chart 9. Real Wage Developments: International Comparison
(1987=100)

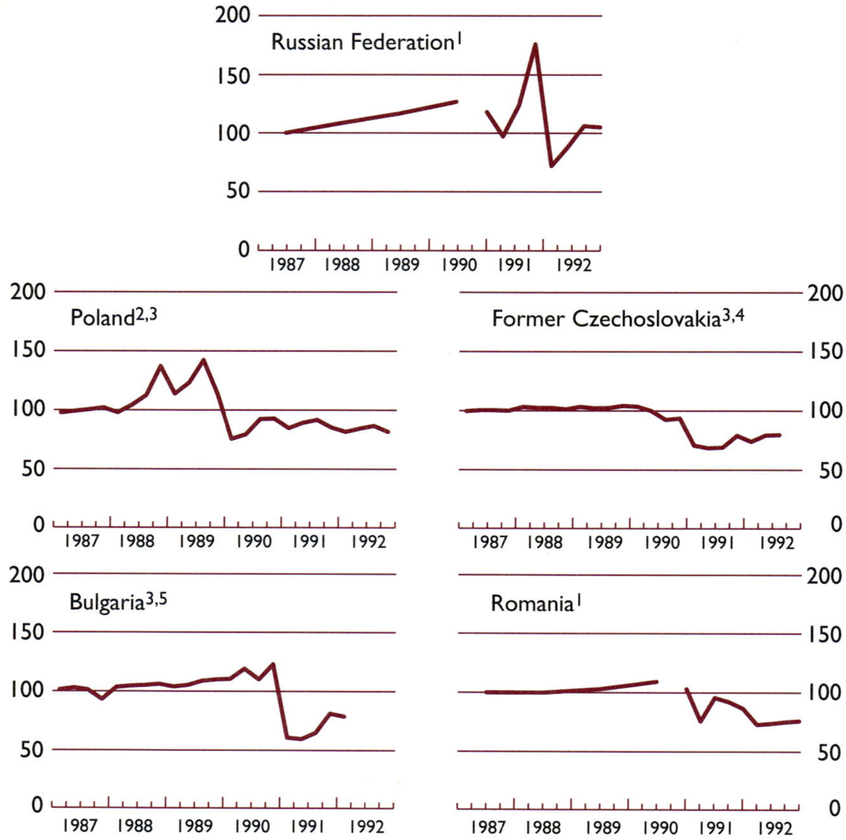

Sources: IMF, *International Financial Statistics*; Goskomstat of the Russian Federation; Polish Central Statistical Office; and Bulgarian national Bank.
[1]Average wage in the national economy.
[2]Average wage in the main areas of the socialized sector (excluding agriculture and state organs).
[3]Seasonally adjusted.
[4]Wage in the socialized sector (excluding agricultural cooperatives).
[5]Average wage in the state sectors.

and East European countries in Chart 9.[44] Because the managers of state enterprises might otherwise lack incentives or the ability to restrain wage increases, such a policy was thought particularly important, both to avoid gradual decapitalization of enterprises through excessive real wages, and/or to provide a nominal anchor for the economy. In Poland, for example, wage bill ceilings were set, and payments in excess were subject to heavy penalties.[45]

The Russian authorities opted for a much weaker incomes policy, whereby the wage bill in excess of four times the minimum wage (times the number of employees) could not be deducted in calculating the taxable profits of an enterprise. Clearly, the effec-

[44] See, for example, Bruno (1992).

[45] Enterprises were permitted to choose between ceilings on the average wage and ceilings on the wage bill; most chose the latter.

Chart 10. Dollar Wage in 1992
(In U.S. dollars per month)[1]

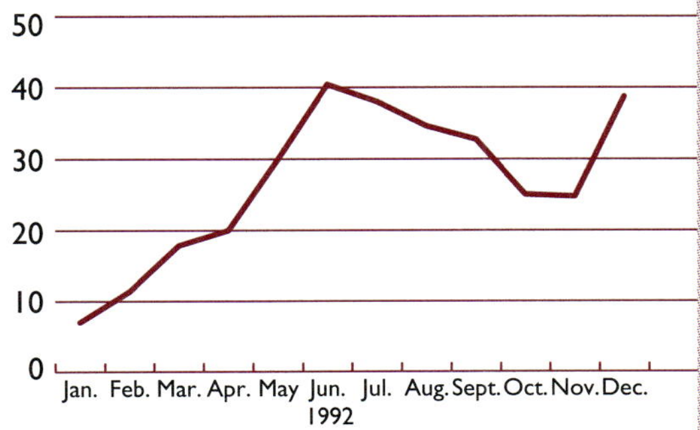

Sources: Goskomstat of the Russian Federation; and Moscow Interbank Currency Exchange.
[1]Average wage in the national economy divided by the average monthly interbank exchange rate.

tiveness of such a policy depends on both the profit tax rate and the setting of the official minimum wage. The setting of the minimum wage was fairly restrictive. After a 90 percent increase in January 1992, the monthly minimum wage was held constant at rub 342, despite rapid inflation, until May 1992, when it was raised to rub 900; this level was then maintained through the rest of the calendar year.[46] On the other hand, the prevailing profit tax rate of 32 percent does not seem prohibitive. Another factor that may have weakened the effectiveness of the policy was that it was not binding on those enterprises that would have earned negative profits even if they had paid an average wage equal to only four times the minimum wage. Moreover, and perhaps more important, the effectiveness of the policy also depended on the perceived "hardness" of the budget constraints faced by enterprises. If enterprises could borrow from the banking system at negative real interest rates, this scheme would be unlikely to deter them from paying "excessive" wages.

Indeed, Russia's wage policy did not induce enterprises to keep most wages below four times the minimum wage. By April 1992, just before the minimum wage was increased, the average wage in industry had reached 11 times the minimum wage (in the final quarter of 1991, it had been less than 6 times the minimum wage). By December 1992, the average wage in industry was more than 20 times the minimum wage. The policy appears to have raised revenue for the Government, but it evidently did not provide a nominal anchor. Monthly wage inflation ran at an average of 28 percent through the first half of 1992, and at 21 percent in the second half.

Money Incomes

It is also of interest to consider, in addition to average wages, a broader measure of household incomes (Table 11). Growth rates of money incomes and average wages had been similar during 1988–90.[47] Not surprisingly, given the large share of wages in money incomes, the growth of money incomes also accelerated in 1991, with the largest part of the increase occurring in the final quarter. However, money incomes rose even faster than wages in 1991, possibly in part as a result of the various types of compensation granted to families with young children, students, pensioners, and savers in the context of the April 1991 price reform. In the first half of 1992, rapid growth of nominal household incomes continued, but the 1991 pattern was reversed: the growth rate of money incomes fell significantly behind that of the average wage, as an abrupt divergence occurred in January 1992 that was not later offset. With the January price burst, measured real money incomes plummeted to only 51 percent of their 1987 level.

The initial shock to household income thus appears to have been considerably greater than indicated by the average wage data. Wage arrears are one factor behind this divergence, since Goskomstat money incomes data are meant to reflect only actual payments. Furthermore, anecdotal evidence suggests that payments arrears may have been proportionately more significant for nonwage income. With the clearing of the bulk of the arrears during the summer, a narrowing of the divergence of the wage and household incomes series would have been expected. Indeed, the growth rate of money incomes averaged 26 percent a month in the second half of 1992, notably exceeding that of wages.

A second reason underlying the slower growth of money incomes than of wages is the slower expansion of some categories of nonwage incomes in 1992. On average, wages rose elevenfold in 1992 over 1991, while pensions increased eightfold and student stipends only fivefold.

Finally, the divergence in 1992 of the household incomes and wage series is likely to have resulted also from measurement problems imparting a down-

[46] The minimum wage was increased to rub 2,250 in January 1993.

[47] See Table 8 in International Monetary Fund (1992).

ward bias on the monthly money incomes series. As noted, these are derived by Goskomstat as the sum of estimates of household saving and household expenditure. The latter, which is mainly based on reports of state retail organizations, was probably underestimated in 1992, implying a corresponding underestimation of incomes.

Sectoral Income Developments

Wage Differentiation Across Activities and Firms

A pattern emerged in sectoral wage developments (Table 13 and Chart 11) that implied a marked widening of the traditional sectoral distribution of income. Sectors that historically exceeded the national average wage tended to experience faster wage growth, while growth was slower in sectors with wages traditionally lower than the national average. For example, industrial wages exceeded the national average by 7 percent in 1987 and by 9 percent in 1991, but by 15 percent in 1992. In the transport sector, the relative wage rose from a traditional 119 percent in 1991 to 144 percent in 1992. On the other hand, wages in agriculture, which in 1987 equaled the national average, fell from 88 percent of the national average wage in 1991 to 71 percent in 1992. In the sciences, the decline was from 104 percent in 1987 to 93 percent in 1991 and to 74 percent in 1992.

Within the industrial sector, relative wage dispersion widened even more. For example, wages in the oil extraction, coal, and gas sectors, which on average all stood at about 160 percent of the national average in 1987, rose respectively to 300, 290, and 380 percent of the national wage in 1992. In December 1992, the average wage in the gas industry came close to rub 75,000, that is, 460 percent of the average wage in the economy, while the average wage in the oil extraction sector exceeded rub 53,000 (or 330 percent) and the average wage in the coal industry was more than rub 39,000 (or 240 percent).[48]

Although the information available is limited, a Goskomstat survey conducted in 1991 suggested that wages of cooperative sector workers and employees at joint ventures exceeded by over one-third those of their counterparts in state enterprises (Gimpelson, 1993). Partial evidence for the early months of 1992 indicates an even wider spread between wages in the emerging private sector and wages in state enterprises.

[48] The sharp rise in relative wages in the energy sector is at variance with the objectives of reversing the decline of investment and raising tax revenues from this sector, which were often used to justify the increases in energy prices.

Chart 11. Wage Structure Across Sectors

(Ratio of sectoral wage to national average wage)

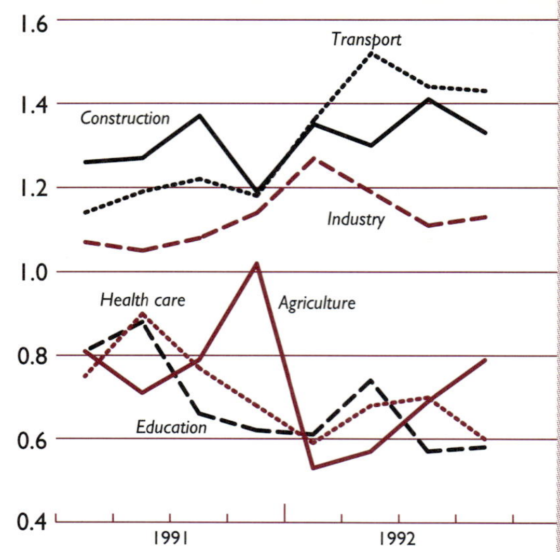

Source: Goskomstat of the Russian Federation.

Regional Wage Dispersion

Like prices, nominal wage levels displayed a significant degree of geographical dispersion in 1992. Chart 12 illustrates the disparities across regions, and shows that wages were roughly 50 percent or more above the national average in the North, Siberia, and the Far East. In part, this resulted from institutionalized wage supplements granted to workers in these areas.[49] Consistent with wage differentiation across branches of activity, wages were even higher in the oil-producing Tiumen *oblast* (close to three times the national average). The growth rates of nominal wages also differed substantially across areas (from a year-on-year increase of 7 times in the Dagestan Republic to an increase of 17 times in the Tiumen *oblast*), suggesting that geographical differences became more pronounced in 1992. In real terms, however, the regional disparities may be less pronounced than the nominal magnitudes suggest, since, as discussed earlier, price levels also vary considerably across areas and are relatively high for many goods in the North, Siberia, and the Far East.

[49] See Barr (1992), p. 50.

Chart 12. Regional Wage Dispersion in 1992
(Wage level in percent of national average)

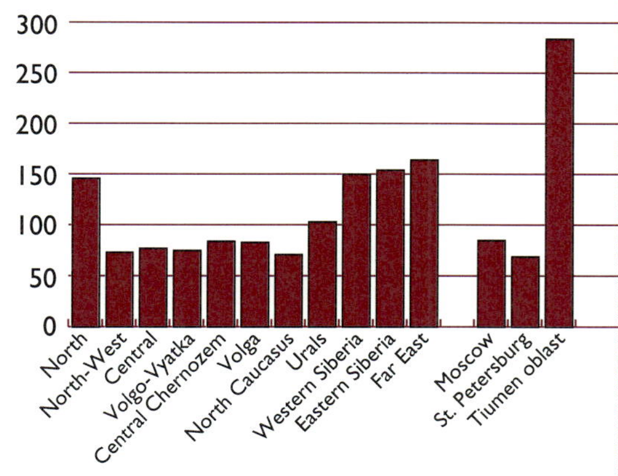

Source: Goskomstat of the Russian Federation.

Minimum Wage

The minimum wage had averaged about 35 percent of the national average wage during 1987–89, but declined to 24 percent in 1991 and then to only 11 percent in 1992. In significant contrast to the extraordinary buildup of overall average wages and household incomes, the minimum wage had failed to grow at all in real terms from 1987 through 1991 (Chart 7). Although it was raised from rub 180 to rub 342 in January 1992, the jump in the price level in that month brought it to only two-fifths of its real 1987 level. Unchanged through the first four months of 1992, it had by April fallen to one-fourth of its real 1987 value. Beginning in May, the minimum wage was raised to rub 900 in certain sectors; this increase applied to all sectors as of July 1. Despite this increase, it averaged only a third of its real 1987 level during the second half of 1992.

Although the relative and absolute positions of those receiving the official minimum wage deteriorated sharply, such individuals represented a very small share of total employment in 1992.[50] However, the official minimum wage is also of interest for its various benchmark roles: for example, as stipulated in the October 24, 1991 law, "On Indexation of Monetary Incomes and Savings of Citizens in the Russian Soviet Federated Socialist Republic," the minimum pension and other social benefits have been linked to the minimum wage;[51] also, as discussed earlier, the minimum wage plays a role in determining the excess wage tax liability of enterprises.

Budgetary Wages

Wages in the budgetary sphere were increased in discrete steps: by 90 percent in December 1991, 45 percent in February 1992, and 80 percent in June, implying that a significant deterioration relative to other wage earners occurred between December 1991 and the second quarter of 1992. The wages of those employed in the budgetary sphere, as occurred with the minimum wage, may not have surged in 1991, leaving these employees without a cushion to absorb the 1992 price burst. Strongly suggestive of a relative deterioration in the position of budgetary sphere workers was the fact that 98 percent of all strikes that occurred during the first five months of 1992 were in the so-called nonproductive sphere, with nearly 90 percent occurring in April and May.[52]

A "unified rate scale" for budgetary wages was introduced in October 1992, involving a base wage subject to periodic adjustment, and a set of coefficients determining wages at the successive echelons as multiples of the base wage. The base wage, which is the minimum wage in the budgetary sphere, was raised in the process by 50 percent, to rub 1,350 a month. The next increase, by one-third and to rub 1,800, took place in December 1992.[53] The cumulative increase in budgetary wages was much smaller, from the fourth quarter of 1991 to end-1992, than the cumulative rise in the average economy-wide wage (10 versus 19 times comparing December 1992 with November 1991).

Pensions

Pension payments have traditionally constituted a significant portion of total household incomes; they amounted to 13 percent of money incomes in 1990. As noted, the minimum pension was linked to the official minimum wage. Indeed, the minimum pension used to be the one received by a large proportion of pensioners, though often with supplementary payments in 1992 (special compensation payments to pensioners amounted to rub 200–300 a month through July 1992, and to rub 420 a month from

[50] Moreover, survey evidence indicates that 90 percent of the minimum wage recipients in urban areas are not the main breadwinner in the household.

[51] A detailed description of the system of cash benefits as of mid-1992 is provided in Barr (1992).

[52] This may also have been related to the accumulation of larger wage arrears in the budgetary sector.

[53] It was raised by 25 percent, to rub 2,250, in February 1993.

August to October 1992). Thus, although the minimum wage—and minimum pension—remained at rub 342 a month in April 1992, the average pension in that month amounted to rub 738, including supplementary payments. In May 1992, the minimum pension was raised to rub 900, and all pensions were revalued (by half a percentage point for each year of seniority). As a result, the average pension increased to rub 1,383 in that month. The percentage increase in the average pension from late 1991 to mid-1992 was similar to that of the overall average wage. The critical difference was that with pensions, no cushion had been accumulated prior to the January price burst: pension increases had not kept up with wage increases in 1991.[54] Furthermore, arrears on pension payments may have been relatively larger than arrears on wage payments in the spring of 1992.

For the second half of 1992, the minimum pension was raised (ahead of the minimum wage) to rub 2,250 in November.[55] In real terms, the minimum pension (including supplementary payments) stood at somewhat over half its 1987 level throughout 1992. Therefore, it declined much less than the minimum wage, but much more than the average wage in the economy. Finally, owing to the revaluation that took place in the spring of 1992, the average pension probably declined less than the minimum pension in 1992.

Income Distribution

The evolution of the distribution of the population by income brackets is presented in Table 14. The distribution as a whole naturally shifted over time as the price level and nominal incomes rose, with the mode for income per capita increasing from less than rub 200 a month in 1990 to almost rub 350 in 1991, to close to rub 1,100 in the first quarter of 1992, and to over rub 4,500 by November 1992. Income dispersion measures point to a widening of income disparities since 1991. The ratio of the average per capita income in the highest decile to the average per capita income in the lowest decile rose steadily from 5.4 in 1991 (and 4.8 in 1990) to 8.7 by December 1992. The Gini coefficient also increased almost monotonically from 0.26 in 1991 (and 0.23 in 1990) to 0.33 by December 1992.[56] The underlying data capture only officially recorded incomes, however. If other income sources grew faster, or differently across groups (as is likely), actual income distribution profiles may have been significantly different.

Summary information on the distribution of wages is published occasionally. As the sectoral wage data suggest, the evidence indicates increasing wage dispersion: by September 1992, the average wage of the highest decile of wage earners had risen to eleven times that of the lowest decile, compared with only six times in September 1991, and almost five and a half times in 1991 as a whole. Preliminary information suggests that the dispersion widened further in the last quarter of 1992.

Poverty

The sharp drop in average measured real incomes following price liberalization suggests that the proportion of the population below any fixed definition of the poverty line increased in early 1992. Indeed, Goskomstat (1992) reported that the proportion of the population receiving incomes less than the minimum income level rose from 35 percent to 50 percent between 1990 and end-1991, and to 80 percent in January 1992. However, an alternative figure was cited by some government officials of a monthly "physiological minimum" of rub 550 in January 1992, implying that about 20 percent of the population was then living below this definition of the poverty line.[57]

Several problems arise in quantifying poverty developments. On the one hand, the sample used in the traditional measure of poverty excludes households other than those of working or retired workers and employees, implying a likely understatement of actual poverty levels.[58] On the other hand, the composition of the associated minimum consumption basket corresponds to a certain desirable standard of living rather than to some notion of a subsistence level, thus entailing an overstatement of poverty.[59]

A new minimum consumption basket was developed in 1992 by Goskomstat and the Ministry of Labor, in collaboration with the World Bank and the World Health Organization, which was inter alia intended to help identify the recipients of targeted

---

[54] This conclusion follows from the historical link of most pensions to the minimum wage, whose real behavior was discussed above.

[55] The minimum pension was further increased to rub 4,275 in February 1993.

[56] See Center of Economic Analysis and Forecasting (1993, pp. 93–94). Such measures cannot be accurately computed on the basis of the highly aggregated information presented in Table 14. They were reportedly derived directly from the raw data.

[57] See the interview with Yevgeniy Gontmakher in *Rossiyskaya Gazeta*, February 25, 1992.

[58] Mitigating this effect somewhat is the likelihood that such a sample also ignores various high-income groups.

[59] See Barr (1992). This bias may have been somewhat offset, however, by the apparent exclusive use of state store prices in valuing the items of the minimum consumption basket, even for those that were largely unavailable at state stores.

social assistance programs.[60] It was based on a different diet (less meat and milk, and more bread, vegetables, and fruits), a higher share of expenditures devoted to foodstuffs, and a more representative sample of households.

The cost of the minimum monthly food basket defined in this context amounted to rub 694 in April 1992 on average (rub 734 for working-age males, and rub 580 for pensioners).[61] One way to infer an overall cost of subsistence is to evaluate the share of food expenses in the relevant household group. Using 80 percent, as suggested by Popkin, Mozhina, and Baturin (1992), implies an average cost of subsistence of about rub 870 in April 1992. Using 68 percent, as did the Ministry of Labor (*Trud*, October 17, 1992), implies an average cost of subsistence of about rub 1,100. These magnitudes compared with an average wage in April 1992 of rub 3,052, an average per capita income of close to rub 1,900,[62] and a minimum wage of rub 342 (revised to rub 900 from May).[63] In August 1992, the cost of the minimum monthly food basket amounted to rub 1,276 and the implied cost of subsistence to either rub 1,595 or rub 1,868 (depending on the share allowed for food).[64] By November 1992, the cost of the minimum monthly food basket had reached rub 2,356, and the implied cost of subsistence rub 2,945 and rub 3,450, respectively.[65] Thus, on this measure, between one-fourth and one-third of the population was living below the poverty line toward the end of 1992.

The disaggregated results of the first survey based on the new minimum consumption basket indicate that the incidence of poverty was highest for households with three or more children, single-parent, female-headed households with young children, and households affected by unemployment or with a disabled family member, as well as for Russian refugees from other states of the former Soviet Union, released prisoners, and the homeless.

Welfare comparisons between the periods before and after price liberalization are difficult, not least because real incomes prior to 1992 were overstated because money incomes were not freely convertible into goods and services and shortages may not have uniformly affected the population. For example, pensioners or others who had more time available to stand in queues were relatively better off before price liberalization than their money incomes suggested.

[60] See Popkin, Mozhina, and Baturin (1992).

[61] The cost of an alternative 19-item minimum food basket defined for an able-bodied working male of 45, and monitored by the Center of Economic Analysis and Forecasting, amounted to rub 883 in April 1992.

[62] Excluding the deposit compensation that became available in that month. This series is likely to be substantially downward biased.

[63] In April, 8.5 percent of the population received a per capita income of less than rub 900, and 17.9 percent an income of less than rub 1,100; 2.4 percent of wage earners received a monthly wage of less than rub 600, and 10.8 percent a monthly wage of less than rub 1,200.

[64] In August, 16.6 percent of the population received an income of less than rub 1,500 and 31.5 percent an income of less than rub 2,000. The high concentration of incomes in the rub 1,500–2,000 bracket implies that the estimate of the percentage of "poor" in the total population will be very sensitive to the choice of the share of income to be spent on food.

[65] In November, 23.6 percent of the population received an income of less than rub 3,000 and 32.5 percent an income of less than rub 3,500.

IV Household Expenditure and Saving

The emergence of substantial open inflation in 1991, the surge in measured real incomes in that year, the anticipated price jumps of April 1991 and January 1992, and the fall in measured real incomes in 1992 have significantly affected recent household expenditure and saving behavior. As discussed in Section III, measured real wages and incomes may be a poor indicator of consumer welfare, particularly when making comparisons with periods when incomes were not readily convertible into goods and services. It is therefore of interest to consider a more direct indicator—the path of real expenditures on goods and services.[66] Similarly, the behavior of the household saving rate is of interest. With the apparent elimination of the monetary overhang and forced saving in early 1992, the measured saving rate might have been expected to drop significantly.

Household Expenditure Behavior

Structure of Consumption

The composition of recorded consumer expenditures continued to shift toward food items in 1992, with their share reaching 43 percent on average for families of workers and employees, up from 37 percent in 1991 (Table 4). (The share of food recorded in 1991 was itself already well above the 1990 level.) Such an increase must reflect the very significant increase in the relative price of food items discussed in Section III, which more than offset the substantial decreases reported in the volume of consumption of major food items.[67] The share of services fell from 9.9 percent in 1991 to 8.3 percent in 1992, while the share of alcohol dropped from 3.9 percent to 3.5 percent. Consumption of other nonfood items declined from 49 percent in 1991 to 45 percent in 1992. A parallel but more pronounced structural shift was observed for families of pensioners, which already spent 61 percent of their income on foodstuffs in 1991: this share increased to 77 percent in 1992.

Developments in Overall Expenditure

The Goskomstat series for nominal household expenditures on goods and services rose continuously throughout 1991 and 1992 (Table 11). However, in real terms, the level of expenditures fluctuated considerably. Chart 13 shows the relationships in 1991–92 between real wages, real expenditures on goods, and inventories in retail trade. Before the preannounced price jumps of April 1991 and January 1992, consumers stepped up their purchases of goods, apparently hoarding considerable quantities. Corresponding to these expenditure surges were sharp declines in retail inventories.[68] Thus, the desire of consumers to hoard tended to outweigh the contrary motivation of retailing enterprises to cling to inventories at such times.

After both price jumps, consumer purchases in real terms dropped considerably. Following the April 1991 reform, however, real purchases recovered rapidly, possibly reflecting the depletion of household stocks, the rapid subsequent catch-up of real incomes and then, toward the end of 1991, the incentive to hoard again in advance of the preannounced general liberalization of prices. In contrast, after the January 1992 price jump, real purchases of goods recovered more slowly and by much less. Real expenditures by households dropped in January to only 42 percent of their 1987 level. As real wages recovered strongly in the first half of 1992, real expenditures also grew, but by June they were still only about one-half their 1987 level.[69] Expenditures

[66] Household expenditures may differ significantly from consumption during periods of extensive hoarding and dishoarding. However, reliable information on total household inventories does not appear to be available.

[67] From 1990 to 1992, for example, the following declines in recorded consumption were observed: meat, 19 percent; milk and dairy products, 25 percent; eggs, 12 percent; vegetables, 8 percent; fish, 36 percent.

[68] The negative correlation between expenditures and inventories that is apparent in Chart 13 partly reflects the measurement of inventories in terms of turnover days.

[69] As is clear from Chart 13, a strong positive relationship existed between changes in real wages and changes in real expenditures; their association in terms of levels was less strong, however, as discussed below.

Chart 13. Wages, Purchases, and Inventories in Retail Trade

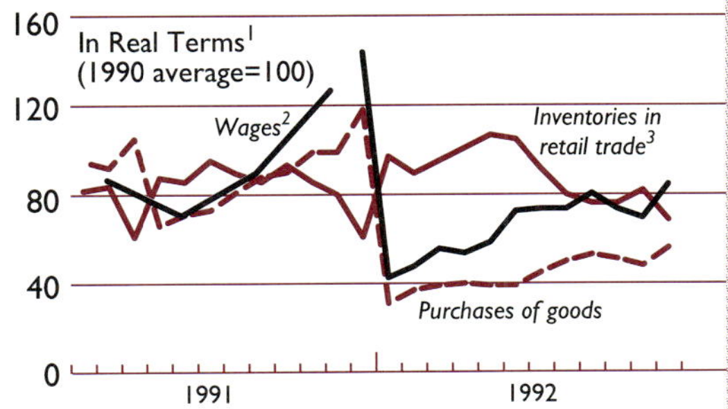

Sources: Goskomstat; and authors' calculations.
[1]The deflator used is a spliced goods price index.
[2]Average monthly wage in the economy; quarterly in 1991, monthly in 1992.
[3]In days of turnover.

grew further in the third quarter, paralleled by a sharp decline in inventories in retail trade. Still, by the final quarter of the year they averaged less than two-thirds of their 1987 level.

Overall food consumption declined markedly in 1992 compared with 1991, and according to some estimates reverted to the level prevailing in the mid-1970s (Center of Economic Analysis and Forecasting, 1993, p.88).

Assessing Expenditure Decline

It was to be expected that real expenditures would fall significantly in early 1992 relative to their surge before the announced price liberalization. The persistence during the remainder of 1992 of a low level of real expenditures relative to the 1987 base might seem more surprising. For the first half of the year, much of the decline in real expenditure can be related to the decline in real incomes, particularly given the wage and other payments arrears. However, the average real wage had reattained its 1987 level by midyear, and generally remained above that level thereafter (although the recovery of other forms of income was weaker). In this connection, the significant increase in indirect taxation in 1992 is relevant: ceteris paribus, such an increase would be expected to crowd out real household expenditure.[70] Also, some of the decline may reflect measurement error; as mentioned earlier, the share of actual consumer expenditures captured by official expenditure data may have declined sharply in early 1992. Also relevant are questions related to the wealth effect of price liberalization and the saving behavior of households, including the role of the inflation tax, which are addressed below.

Even if overstated by the official data, it is likely that a significant decline in real consumer expenditure did occur in 1992. Viewed from the production side, such a decline may a priori seem necessitated by the cumulative decline in aggregate output, as, by 1992, real net material product (NMP) had fallen by more than one-fourth from its 1987 level and was down 20 percent over 1991. Under those circumstances, the fall in net exports that would have been required to maintain absorption would have been enormous. However, the production of consumer goods (food and nonfood) fell less than overall NMP in 1991 (by 15 percent), and had grown much faster than overall output since 1987. As a result, output of consumer goods in 1992 remained about 6 percent above its 1987 level. On that account, a decline in the consumption of goods compared with 1991 is indeed likely, but not compared with 1987.[71]

As regards the impact of the decline in expenditure on consumer welfare, a number of qualifying points are relevant. First, in the short run, the level of expenditure may have partially reflected households' temporary reliance on consuming stocks of goods accumulated before January 1992. Without reliable information on household inventories, it is difficult to gauge the importance of this factor, but presumably it declined over time. Second, the apparent loss in welfare from lower real expenditures must be offset to some extent by the reduced time that consumers spent in queues.[72] Similarly, consumers in 1992 were better able to choose the composition of their consumption basket freely, whereas before price liberalization a significant portion of their expenditures may have represented "spillover" demand (demand for goods that happened to be available but that offered only very low marginal utility per ruble spent).

Saving Behavior

Methodology

In reviewing developments in saving, this section focuses on the household monetary saving data prepared by Goskomstat and presented in the table,

[70] The accuracy of measurement of real expenditures should not be influenced by the introduction of the VAT. The household expenditure data include payment of the VAT, and, correspondingly, the price indices used here to deflate this series are based on VAT-inclusive prices.

[71] If the necessary information were available, stockbuilding and net exports of consumer goods would also have to be taken into account.

[72] See, for example, Roberts (1992).

"Money Incomes and Expenditures of the Population," as well as on information on the stocks of household money balances. Household saving in Russia has traditionally been largely monetary in nature. In contrast to Western economies, for example, private holdings of such assets as real estate and enterprise shares were generally not available as forms in which to hold wealth. One additional channel that was relevant was the stockpiling of goods, but as noted earlier this must be disregarded for lack of quantified information. Also, without sufficient information—particularly the complete lack of data on cash holdings—foreign currency assets are largely ignored here. However, as such assets may constitute a significant proportion of households' total financial wealth when valued at market exchange rates, they should not be completely overlooked.

Also important—and worthy of some digression as one of the more intriguing developments of late 1992—was the issuance of vouchers for the mass privatization of large-scale Russian industry. Every Russian citizen was entitled to one voucher; their distribution began on October 1, 1992, and most had been received by year-end. As the face value of a privatization voucher was rub 10,000, the entire stock of vouchers had a face value of roughly rub 1.5 trillion. Although the market value of such assets in real terms should in principle be immune from inflationary erosion, in fact, even the nominal market value of a voucher declined, from about rub 9,000 in early October to about rub 5,500 at end-December 1992 (the market price of vouchers tended to fluctuate with the political debate concerning the conditions and scope of their use). At this price, the stock of vouchers at year-end—including undistributed vouchers and those that had already been used to purchase shares—was worth about one-third of household ruble money balances, the form of household wealth emphasized in the following discussion. Indeed, the case of privatization vouchers may be instructively contrasted with other forms of saving and wealth. In fact, their issuance does not represent a form of saving at all, just as it does not represent an addition to the wealth of society as a whole: essentially, vouchers represent a mechanism for redistributing existing aggregate wealth. Of course, a voucher does represent wealth to its individual holder, who at issuance sees the abstract claim on Russian industry in general that he previously held in principle being converted into a potentially marketable and certainly more liquid claim.

Developments

The accelerating growth of the household saving rate has been considered a prime indicator of the increasing repressed inflation and monetary overhang before the price liberalization in January 1992.[73] In 1985, financial saving out of disposable income was little more than 5 percent, but it grew steadily to 9 percent in 1988, and then reached nearly 13 percent in 1990. The acceleration continued in 1991, with the saving rate reaching 25 percent by June. A new peak was reached in December 1991, when the expected short-term real rate of return on financial assets must have been extremely negative. Despite the strong incentive to hoard goods that resulted in a surge of expenditures, saving out of disposable income jumped to 32 percent in the final month of 1991. It is difficult to avoid concluding that a large share of this saving was involuntary.

Simply by ending the phenomenon of forced saving, the liberalization of most prices in January 1992 might have been expected to lower the saving rate significantly. The increase in indirect taxation might also have induced households to lower their rate of saving, if they sought to avoid the full implied reduction in their real expenditures. On the other hand, there could be no presumption that the saving rate would fall back entirely to historical levels, particularly as structural changes may have made them irrelevant.

The measured saving rate did fall somewhat in the first quarter of 1992, but only in comparison with its December 1991 peak (Table 11). The saving rate rose anew at the end of the second quarter of 1992, and monthly rates of saving out of disposable income averaged about 35 percent during the second half of 1992.[74] However, the measurement issue is again relevant: it is likely that the measured saving rate is biased upward.[75]

Comparison with Other Transition Economies

In several Central and East European economies price liberalization also did not lead to a fall in the measured saving rate. On the contrary, in Poland it jumped with the liberalization of food prices in August 1989; after falling somewhat, it then peaked at nearly 30 percent in early 1990. In the former Czechoslovakia, the circumstances prior to the price

[73] See, for example, International Monetary Fund and others (1991), Vol. 1, Chap. III.3, which notes that financial saving out of disposable income had remained fairly stable for more than 20 years until the late 1980s.

[74] The April 1992 spike reflects the unfreezing of rub 71.9 billion in demand deposits and the July 1992 spike, the large payments of wage and other arrears to households.

[75] This follows from the fact that the expenditure data are probably biased downward. Since the monthly incomes data are estimated from expenditure data, the same bias would appear in the incomes data, thus biasing the ratio of expenditure to income downward (and the saving rate upward).

reform were quite different from those in Russia, as households had not been granted enormous increases in nominal incomes. Accordingly, the saving rate actually became negative in the quarter before price liberalization, as households apparently anticipated higher prices. After prices were liberalized, the saving ratio was little changed in the first quarter, but then rose significantly, peaking at almost 20 percent in the fourth quarter of 1991. In Bulgaria, the saving ratio remained fairly stable in the late 1980s, falling only slightly in 1990, while in 1991 saving out of disposable income rose from less than 9 percent to more than 13 percent. Only in Romania was a fall in the saving rate observed. It had approximately doubled in 1989 and again in 1990, exceeding 12 percent of gross income in 1990, but fell back to about 7 percent in the first three quarters of 1991.

Only in Poland was the level of the post-reform saving rate at all near that of Russia. In Poland, however, it fell sharply in the second quarter after comprehensive price liberalization. As discussed below, the higher rate of saving observed in Russia is consistent with the fact that higher inflation, other things being equal, implies a higher inflation tax on household money balances.

Explaining Higher Saving in 1992

One factor that might have exerted upward pressure on saving in 1992 in Russia was a greater precautionary motive, in a context of heightened uncertainty about future employment and income prospects. Indeed, employment security and the traditional provision of most "life-cycle" services by the state were presumably responsible for the fairly low rate of household saving that had existed before the late 1980s.[76] Yet even if the desired level of the real stock of savings did rise with the beginning of the transition to a market economy, the actual real stock that existed in late 1991 was presumably even higher than this amount, as suggested by the January 1992 price jump. Thus a greater precautionary motive does not in itself explain greater saving in 1992; it must be assumed in addition that the price level overshot, bringing the real stock of savings below the (perhaps newly higher) desired level.

The real stock of household monetary savings was drastically reduced in early 1992 (Chart 14). With the January 1992 price burst, household real money balances declined by almost 75 percent.[77]

Chart 14. Household Balances

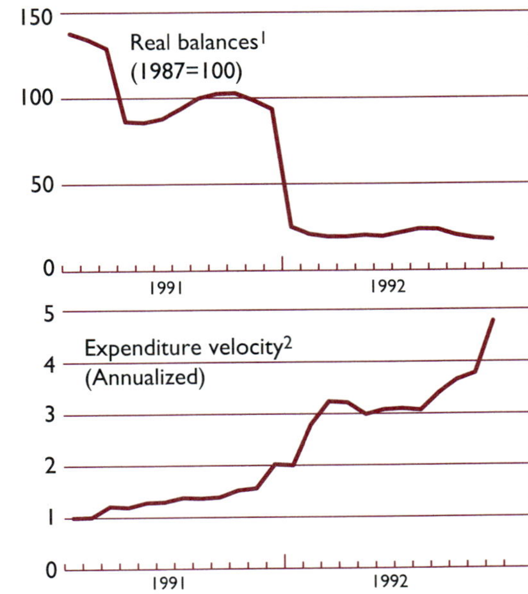

Sources: Goskomstat of the Russian Federation; and authors' calculations.

[1]The frozen rub 71.9 billion of deposit compensation are imputed as an addition to household deposits in April 1992. Holdings of foreign exchange are not included.

[2]Household expenditures on goods and services over average household money holdings in the period (excluding foreign exchange holdings).

Presumably most, if not all, of this decline represented elimination of excess or undesired real balances. Nevertheless, it is possible that the price level overshot in aggregate, in the sense of real balances being reduced beyond the desired level.

Such overshooting is not implausible a priori; after all, it is difficult to see what mechanism would have ensured that the Russian price level would jump, particularly in the short run, by an amount close to that needed to equate desired and actual real balances.[78] In the short run, prices may not always reflect monetary equilibrium, as time may be needed before errors become obvious, or as prices are set on the basis of expectations that may or may not turn out to be correct. In Russia, limited pricing experience and a high degree of monopolization

[76] See International Monetary Fund and others (1991).

[77] Again, this refers to ruble holdings only. However, an illustrative calculation using the black market exchange rate suggests that if foreign currency assets of households were as large as, say, $10 billion in late 1991, then total household real balances would still have dropped by more than half between mid-October 1991 (i.e., on the eve of the announcement of price liberalization) and end-January 1992.

[78] Similarly, undershooting was in principle also a possibility.

may also have played a role.[79] The meaningfulness of the concept of monetary equilibrium in a context of dubious budget constraints and rapid growth of arrears can also be debated.[80]

Assuming that the Russian price level did indeed overshoot in January 1992, households might have been expected to save subsequently at a high rate, to raise their real balances. If so, they were unsuccessful, as price-setters evidently did not respond to the signal of reduced aggregate demand in the following months. The expansion of interenterprise and bank credit to some degree permitted firms to continue to raise prices despite limited final demand and to pile up inventories of unsold output. Household real balances continued to fall, dropping a further 22 percent by the end of the first quarter, despite a saving rate that was high by historical standards. (In February 1992, consumer prices grew such that households, to maintain their real balances at the January level, would have had to save more than 80 percent of their gross income in that month.) Indeed, a difficulty with the overshooting hypothesis is the apparent failure of its implicit prediction of a subsequent strong recovery of real balances. Such a recovery did not occur in 1992 (Chart 14 and Table 15).[81] Persistent overshooting over such a longer horizon seems less plausible.

The alternative assumption of continuous stock equilibrium may also yield insight into 1992 developments, with the high saving rate seen as primarily reflecting the inflation tax on household real balances. Suppose that in January 1992 the price level adjusted to bring desired and actual real balances broadly in line. Thus the January price burst eliminated excess real balances; in the remainder of the first quarter, adaptation to an inflationary environment then brought down desired and actual real balances somewhat further. In the second quarter, however, these real balances became relatively stable, perhaps as households found it difficult immediately to economize further on real balances or felt it imprudent to lower their stock of savings any more. Real balances did then rise somewhat in the third quarter as inflation slowed, but this increase was more than reversed by a decline in the fourth quarter as inflation accelerated strongly. Thus, while the assumption of continuous stock equilibrium is strong, the path of actual real balances in 1992 does not seem implausible as a path for desired real balances.

According to this line of reasoning, that household real (ruble) balances in the second half of 1992 averaged only about one-fifth of their 1987 level (or that on a per capita basis nominal balances represented only about 1.2 weeks of the current average wage, down from 6 weeks in 1987) may have two explanations. First, in the benchmark year of 1987 excess real balances may have already existed; that is, a monetary overhang had been accumulating already for some time. Second, desired levels of real balances may have fallen dramatically,[82] not least because of the motivation to avoid (partially) the inflation tax present in 1992 but absent in 1987.[83]

Inflation was certainly sufficiently rapid in 1992 to imply a significant tax on Russian households. Abstracting from the very low interest receipts earned on household deposits, even in the third quarter of 1992 (when inflation was least rapid), households would have needed to save about 20 percent of their disposable income each month to preserve the level of real balances they held in the previous month.[84] In the fourth quarter, this figure rose to almost 50 percent as inflation accelerated.[85] Thus the inflation tax on real balances may have been a significant factor underlying the high rates of household saving observed in 1992.

[79] The view that monopolies were somehow responsible for ongoing inflation was prevalent in Russia during 1992. The standard objection is that the degree of monopolization may affect the structure of relative prices but not the rate of inflation. However, some have argued that in Russia extensive monopolization may indeed "cause" inflation, in the sense that monopolies can use threats of mass layoffs to obtain (inflationary) government subsidies.

[80] Yet this point should not be taken too far. Despite imperfectly credible budget constraints, rapid growth of arrears, etc., a finite aggregate price level did exist at each moment during 1992. Money had value in Russia in 1992, and hyperinflation (by the conventional definition) was avoided.

[81] Among other information, Table 15 presents the estimated stock of real household balances according to a 1987 = 100 index. This calibration is arbitrary and is not meant to suggest that the stock of such balances in that year represented an equilibrium or desired level.

Taking foreign currency deposits into account would complicate the picture: although such holdings apparently increased during 1992, the ruble exchange rate appreciated considerably in real terms after January 1992.

[82] Taking into account the stock of foreign currency holdings would most likely reduce the gap between the 1987 and 1992 levels.

[83] Another factor that may have contributed to a decreased willingness to hold ruble assets may have been a perceived possibility of their confiscation, in light of the precedent of the January 1991 monetary reform, which involved the withdrawal from circulation with only partial compensation of large-denomination ruble notes.

[84] In the event, saving rates were higher in the third quarter, averaging 37 percent, as households added to real balances.

[85] The actual saving rate in the fourth quarter was smaller, averaging 33 percent. During this period, inflation accelerated, household real balances fell, and the expenditure velocity of their nominal balances rose significantly (Chart 14). Although the surge in inflation may be largely attributable to the somewhat lagged effect of a significant loosening of financial policies, the possibility cannot be excluded that the issuance of privatization vouchers played a role in households' decisions to hold smaller real balances during the fourth quarter of 1992.

The above discussion abstracted from interest earnings of households. Goskomstat reported that these were rub 93 billion in 1992, or no more than 5 percent of the total increase in nominal household balances recorded during 1992. This amount would also represent only about 8 percent of the estimated average stock of household ruble savings (including cash) in 1992, implying a pathetic rate of return in light of the inflation observed during the period. These low interest earnings reflect both the low nominal interest rates available at the Savings Bank (few commercial banks accepted household deposits in 1992), as well as an increasing tendency to save in the form of cash. Presumably the somewhat less negative real return on deposits was largely offset in the view of most Russian households by the various advantages of holding cash. In sum, available returns on ruble-denominated financial assets offered households very little shelter from the inflation tax in 1992.

Finally, the relatively high measured rate of saving in 1992 may also have reflected persisting shortages. As discussed earlier, price liberalization was not complete, and some shortages were still observed in 1992, suggesting that the forced saving phenomenon may not have ceased entirely.[86]

[86] This effect may not be of great importance. As discussed earlier, shortages in 1992 were likely to be more microeconomic in nature than in 1991: with most prices liberalized, "spillover" demand opportunities are presumably much better than before. Thus a consumer unable to purchase the good yielding the highest marginal utility per ruble may be more likely to purchase a second-best good than simply to give up.

V Concluding Remarks

In considering the aftermath of price liberalization in Russia, a number of essential points emerge from an analysis of the data available for 1992. Some of these findings raise questions of interpretation and issues for future research.

The experience in 1992 should be viewed not in isolation but rather as the belated resolution of a substantial disequilibrium that had been growing through the late 1980s and that worsened dramatically in the final months of 1991. Thus, comparisons with 1991 (frequently encountered in the press) may be particularly misleading. By contrast, this study used 1987 as a benchmark, as the last year before the beginning of a pronounced divergence in wage and price developments. Comparisons with several Central and East European countries provided additional perspective. Finally, the technical aspects, coverage, and limitations of the data presented were discussed, to facilitate future empirical analysis.

On the liberalization of prices, the price jump of January 1992 in Russia far exceeded those registered in Central and Eastern Europe. At the level of individual goods, overshooting of some prices did occur. On the aggregate consumer price level, the question of overshooting remains open. Although the size of the Russian price jump was impressive, the price level in the first month of the liberalization turned out to be similar to that of Poland in January 1990, when considered in relation to the level of real output and of the money stock.[87] Of course, it is possible that the price level overshot in both countries.

Following the January 1992 price jump, CPI inflation dropped sharply, but continued at double-digit monthly levels, in contrast to the aftermath of comprehensive price liberalizations elsewhere. During the summer, the deceleration of inflation was reversed as financial policies were loosened, and by the fourth quarter of 1992 Russia had entered a phase of very high inflation, bordering on and threatening to degenerate into hyperinflation.

[87] That is, money as a share of nominal GDP (alternatively, velocity) was similar in both countries.

The January 1992 jump in industrial producer prices was even larger than that in the CPI. Their sustained faster growth compared with the CPI is one of the more striking and puzzling developments of the first half of 1992. A number of explanations have been suggested, including the possibility that whereas households were subject to credibly hard budget constraints in 1992, the same could not be said of state-owned industrial firms.

Large shifts in relative prices occurred in 1992. In particular, the domestic relative price of food rose significantly. The domestic and international relative price of oil and gasoline increased as well, while that of gas and electricity remained very low.

The increase in the price level not only rationed consumer demand but also induced some response of supply at the retail level. The availability of goods in stores improved drastically, and the rundown of retail inventories was ended. A striking decline was observed in the spread between prices for similar goods in free markets and state stores.

Interpreting these developments, it seems reasonable to conclude that one of the most fundamental effects of the price liberalization was a significant move toward market relations at the retail level. Some shortages were still to be found, partly as a result of incomplete price liberalization, but the generalized "shortage economy" ended abruptly. Money, or at least cash money, became readily convertible for domestic goods and services, thus establishing a basis for an exchange (rather than command or barter) economy. The extent of the supply response at the producer level remains more difficult to assess.

The immediate cause of the disequilibrium that grew through 1991 was an increase in the measured real wage, which was out of proportion to the supply of consumer goods and desired saving. This disequilibrium was substantially but briefly reduced in the second quarter of 1991, only to reach a new—and extreme—level at the end of that year. The price jump of January 1992 then brought the average wage, in real terms, to only about two-thirds of its 1987 level. Whether or not this initial adjustment was excessive, a strong recovery of real wages followed, and by midyear they had climbed beyond their 1987 level. The appropriate level of the real wage is difficult to judge, but the cumulative decline in the aggregate productivity of labor suggests that the real wage may have again become excessive by mid-1992, albeit not to the degree found before price liberalization.

The above conclusion is based on wage data reported by enterprises. From the point of view of Russian households, however, a significant development in 1992 was the growth of wage and other payment arrears. Actual wage payments, for example, were lower than implied by the official wage data, although the bulk of these arrears was cleared in the summer of 1992, when large-denomination ruble notes were put into circulation. Moreover, the wage data do not reflect the significant inflation tax on Russian households during 1992. Such a tax may have played an important role in 1992, ensuring that household demand was consistent with the overall decline in output, despite real wages that may have been excessive by the second half of the year.

Whereas incomes policy was considered an important component of stabilization programs in Central and Eastern Europe, Russia implemented a much weaker policy after its price liberalization. At 32 percent, the rate of taxation on average wages in excess of four times the minimum wage was apparently not prohibitive. The policy clearly failed to provide a nominal anchor, as nominal wage inflation averaged nearly 25 percent a month during 1992. Without macroeconomic policies consistent with low inflation, the relatively weak form of incomes policy implemented in Russia was probably doomed to fail as a complementary nominal anchor.

Developments in average wages and incomes can conceal important changes in the distribution of income, a point that seems to apply to Russia in 1992. Comparisons with periods before 1992 suffer from the problem that measured real money incomes were then not readily convertible into goods. Nevertheless, several observations are possible. The overall distribution of wages widened significantly; some of this change can be seen in an increasing dispersion of average wages across key sectors of the economy. The relative position of persons receiving the minimum wage deteriorated sharply in 1992 (although this cohort was not significant in size). It is also likely that the relative position of pensioners and those employed in the budgetary sphere deteriorated in 1992. The analysis of poverty is complicated by various technical problems. However, the results of a survey based on a new minimum consumption basket suggest that at the end of 1992 as much as one-fourth to one-third of Russians could be classified as poor.

The use of measured real wages and incomes as indicators of changes in consumer welfare is problematic when money in the base period is not readily convertible into goods. The path of real expenditures by households is therefore of interest as a more direct indicator. These expenditures had grown considerably in the late 1980s, and surged in late 1991, as retail inventories were run down. With the January price burst, estimated real expenditures plummeted to about 40 percent of their 1987 level. Some recovery occurred thereafter, supported by the growth of real wages, but by the final quarter of 1992 real household expenditures still averaged less than two-thirds of their 1987 level. It seems likely, however, that the household expenditure data became biased downward in 1992. Whatever was the actual decline in expenditure, its effect on consumer welfare was presumably offset—to some degree—by reliance on previously accumulated stocks and by the reduction of time spent in queues. Similarly, the likelihood that much of previous consumer expenditure represented "spillover" demand is relevant.

The rise in the saving rate in the late 1980s has been considered a prime indicator of growing macroeconomic disequilibrium in that period. The saving rate grew significantly further in 1991, with the surge in nominal incomes and increasing shortages. With the liberalization of prices in 1992 presumably ending the phenomenon of forced saving, the rate of saving might have been expected to fall. However, the measured saving rate in 1992 exceeded even the historically high levels reached in 1991. Interpretation of this finding remains open and includes the possibility that the saving rate implied by the official data has become upwardly biased. It is likely, however, that much of observed household saving corresponds to a significant inflation tax on real balances.

Statistical Appendix

Table 1. Industrial Producer Price Index
(Monthly percentage change unless otherwise specified)

	Dec. 1990	1991 Avg.[1]	Dec. 1991[2]	Jan. 1992	Feb. 1992	Mar. 1992	Apr. 1992	May 1992	June 1992	July 1992	Aug. 1992	Sep. 1992	Oct. 1992	Nov. 1992	Dec. 1992	1992 Avg.[1]	Dec. 1992[2]
Electric energy	. . .	97	110	269	55	49	35	32	92	49	19	5	5	32	17	2,657	5,409
Fuel	. . .	124	129	394	26	28	6	108	228	9	1	5	113	36	20	3,323	9,166
Ferrous metallurgy	. . .	110	237	361	160	25	33	27	24	11	8	4	12	14	7	3,085	3,525
Nonferrous metallurgy	. . .	134	233	500	157	67	12	27	37	42	9	8	26	28	45	2,850	5,120
Chemicals	. . .	109	165	502	78	33	34	25	22	17	8	9	31	22	15	2,293	3,791
Petrochemicals	. . .	103	149	696	37	20	34	16	38	23	8	1	23	33	32	2,894	5,248
Machinery	. . .	117	212	412	63	33	16	15	9	15	16	11	17	28	22	1,739	2,621
Forestry, timber processing, and pulp and paper	. . .	155	242	371	123	26	10	10	12	11	10	5	17	14	23	1,465	2,921
Construction materials	. . .	147	215	382	69	13	15	15	30	22	12	11	29	27	14	1,605	2,714
Light industry	. . .	206	371	230	61	16	6	8	8	7	7	13	11	39	26	874	1,198
Food industry	. . .	161	314	365	25	18	19	9	23	12	14	28	35	27	24	1,722	2,628
Total	. . .	138	236	382	75	28	17	23	36	17	13	14	27	27	20	1,949	3,275

Source: Goskomstat of the Russian Federation.
[1] Year-average increase over previous year.
[2] Percentage increase over December of previous year.

Table 2. Inflation Indicators

(Percentage change over previous period)

		Retail Price Indices					Consumer Price Indices						
							Hybrid CPI					CPI	
	Industrial Producer Prices	Goods and services, all trade	Goods, state and cooperative trade	Goods, city cooperatives	Goods, *kolkhoz* markets	Services	All goods and services	Food goods (excluding alcohol)	Nonfood goods	Services	Alcohol	National urban CPI	Moscow CPI
1987	. . .	. . .	1.6	2.4	3.7	. . .	. . .	. . .	. . .	. . .	. . .	. . .	. . .
1988	. . .	. . .	0.2	0.6	2.5	. . .	. . .	. . .	. . .	. . .	. . .	. . .	. . .
1989	1.2	. . .	2.4	0.5	7.4	. . .	. . .	. . .	. . .	. . .	. . .	. . .	. . .
1990	3.9	5.6	5.2	14.1	34.3	2.1	. . .	. . .	. . .	. . .	. . .	. . .	. . .
1991	138	92.7	95.3	112	132.3	70.6	. . .	. . .	. . .	. . .	. . .	. . .	. . .
1991													
January	62.9	6.2	6.6	17.6	13.2	3.2	6.2	6.3	0.9	3.2	0.4	. . .	. . .
February	18.9	4.9	4.8	14.4	14.9	5.2	4.8	3.7	5.9	5.2	1.6	. . .	. . .
March	7.1	6.3	6.4	7.0	9.3	5.5	6.3	3.9	4.6	5.5	8.6	. . .	. . .
April	8.2	52.2	54.4	38.7	7.5	24.3	63.5	94.3	70.5	21.5	15.3	. . .	. . .
May	3.8	2.5	2.4	−0.8	−5.3	3.5	3.0	0.3	5.4	3.9	0.9	. . .	. . .
June	2.8	0.2	0.0	−1.5	21.2	2.9	1.2	−0.6	2.2	3.5	0.3	. . .	. . .
July	17.5	−0.2	−0.7	−3.1	−20.1	5.5	0.6	−4.2	2.8	4.4	0.8	. . .	. . .
August	15.2	0.1	−0.2	−5.7	−17.7	2.2	0.5	−5.2	4.1	1.9	1.0	. . .	. . .
September	6.6	1.4	1.3	5.3	−4.8	2.2	1.1	−2.9	3.9	1.8	0.7	. . .	. . .
October	5.8	4.2	3.9	11.1	13.5	2.1	3.5	2.8	5.0	2.6	1.0	. . .	. . .
November	9.4	8.6	9.0	27.6	33.2	3.8	8.9	11.8	8.6	3.9	7.6	. . .	. . .
December	11.3	12.0	12.6	49.7	39.3	4.3	12.1	20.4	10.5	3.4	5.3	. . .	. . .
Within year	236.3	146.1	152.1	360.8	281.2	99.7	160.3	171	211	79	52	143.9	203.9
1992													
January	382	233	245	. . .	53	127	245	306	211	130	301	296.0	234.2
February	75	25	24	. . .	15	33	38	20	48	87	10	27.3	31.7
March	28	21	21	. . .	16	16	30	18	42	34	13	16.4	13.7
April	17	15	15	. . .	7	16	22	17	25	31	13	17.2	25.3
May	23	11	11	. . .	5	15	12	11	12	18	11	10.5	23.8
June	36	13	13	. . .	−2	31	19	13	12	39	55	13.9	48.3
July	17	7	7	. . .	−13	25	11	8	10	21	14	7.1	5.4
August	13	7	. . .	. . .	−15	12	9	6	10	11	8	8.6	6.0
September	14	11	. . .	. . .	12	11	12	11	13	11	8	15.2	11.6
October	27	21	. . .	. . .	17	29	23	26	20	29	20	31.1	46.5
November	27	25	. . .	. . .	30	. . .	26	27	26	23	28	27.1	22.5
December	20	26	. . .	. . .	33	. . .	25	26	27	19	25	25.3	18.7
Within year	3,275	. . .	. . .	. . .	731	1,575	2,509	2,033	2,573	3,258	2,373	2,318	2,956

Source: Goskomstat of the Russian Federation.

Table 3. Producer Price Inflation: International Comparison [1]
(Percentage change over previous period)

		Bulgaria	Former Czechoslovakia	Poland	Romania	Russia
	1987	0.7	—	26.7	. . .	. . .
	1988	3.7	0.1	59.8	. . .	. . .
	1989	3.1	−0.7	212.8	. . .	1.2
	1990	5.0	4.4	622.3	. . .	3.9
	1991	. . .	69.9	48.1	. . .	138.1
	1992	. . .	8.6	28.5	. . .	1,949
1989						
	January	. . .	. . .	11.0	. . .	. . .
	February	. . .	. . .	6.1	. . .	. . .
	March	. . .	. . .	5.2	. . .	. . .
	April	. . .	. . .	8.9	. . .	. . .
	May	. . .	. . .	5.9	. . .	. . .
	June	. . .	. . .	6.7	. . .	. . .
	July	. . .	. . .	5.4	. . .	. . .
	August	. . .	. . .	34.4*	. . .	. . .
	September	. . .	. . .	29.5	. . .	. . .
	October	. . .	. . .	43.8*	. . .	. . .
	November	. . .	. . .	34.8	. . .	. . .
	December	. . .	. . .	37.9	. . .	. . .
1990						
	January	. . .	. . .	109.6*	. . .	. . .
	February	. . .	. . .	9.6	1.5	. . .
	March	. . .	. . .	−0.2	—	. . .
	April	. . .	. . .	2.1	—	. . .
	May	. . .	. . .	0.6	2.0	. . .
	June	. . .	. . .	1.5	0.2	. . .
	July	. . .	. . .	3.3	—	. . .
	August	. . .	. . .	2.9	—	. . .
	September	. . .	. . .	2.7	2.4	. . .
	October	. . .	. . .	4.9	4.6	. . .
	November	. . .	. . .	3.6	126.2*	. . .
	December	. . .	. . .	3.3	3.3	. . .
1991						
	January	. . .	24.0*	9.8	4.3	62.9*
	February	118.9*	19.3	5.4	0.6	18.9
	March	13.5	−0.2	1.4	1.1	7.1
	April	1.8	2.9	1.0	16.3*	8.2
	May	14.4	1.7	1.6	3.5	3.8
	June	12.5	−0.8	3.1	1.3	2.8
	July	3.0	−0.5	2.1	7.7	17.3
	August	0.5	0.4	1.6	17.6	15.2
	September	7.5	−0.4	1.6	9.1	6.6
	October	−4.1	—	2.3	11.2	5.8
	November	5.2	0.9	1.1	25.4	9.4
	December	8.0	0.6	0.3	42.7	11.3
1992						
	January	13.3	1.0	3.2	10.1	382*
	February	. . .	1.9	1.9	3.1	75
	March	. . .	0.1	3.3	0.1	28
	April	. . .	0.5	3.1	5.5	17
	May	. . .	1.1	2.0	1.0	23*
	June	. . .	0.5	2.5	0.1	36
	July	. . .	0.6	1.5	. . .	17
	August	. . .	−0.1	2.0	. . .	13
	September	. . .	0.4	2.0	. . .	14*
	October	. . .	0.8	2.8	. . .	27
	November	. . .	0.9	1.8	. . .	27
	December	. . .	0.3	1.6	. . .	20

Sources: IMF, *International Financial Statistics*; OECD (1992); National Bank of Bulgaria, *Annual Reports* and *Bank Review* (2/1992); and Goskomstat of the Russian Federation.

[1] Producer prices in industry; an asterisk denotes a month of major price reform or liberalization.

Table 4. Structure of Consumer Expenditures
(In percent of total expenditures)

	Foodstuffs	Nonfood Goods	Alcohol	Services	Total
		Families of Workers and Employees			
1991					
Year average	37.3	48.9	3.9	9.9	100.0
December	33.7	54.2	3.4	8.7	100.0
1992					
Year average	43.3	44.9	3.5	8.3	100.0
January	47.4	41.1	4.7	6.8	100.0
February	45.8	41.3	4.1	8.8	100.0
March	41.9	45.2	3.5	9.4	100.0
April	41.9	46.8	3.0	8.3	100.0
May	43.6	41.3	3.8	11.3	100.0
June	43.4	42.5	3.2	10.9	100.0
July	38.4	49.8	3.0	8.8	100.0
August	39.1	49.6	3.4	7.9	100.0
September	44.8	44.9	2.9	7.4	100.0
October	44.8	45.6	2.8	6.8	100.0
November	44.5	45.3	3.3	6.9	100.0
December	43.9	45.3	4.4	6.4	100.0
		Families of Pensioned Workers and Employees			
1991					
Year average	61.0	22.3	6.7	10.0	100.0
December	65.7	18.9	5.2	10.2	100.0
1992					
Year average	76.7	10.2	5.7	7.4	100.0
January	71.3	15.8	5.2	7.7	100.0
February	73.7	12.3	7.2	6.8	100.0
March	72.1	10.0	5.8	12.1	100.0
April	69.2	7.2	5.0	18.6	100.0
May	77.8	9.8	4.8	7.6	100.0
June	79.8	7.6	5.9	6.7	100.0
July	78.7	10.2	6.0	5.1	100.0
August	81.0	7.3	6.7	5.0	100.0
September	80.0	10.9	4.9	4.2	100.0
October	77.9	12.6	3.5	6.0	100.0
November	81.0	9.2	5.7	4.1	100.0
December	77.9	9.2	7.6	5.3	100.0

Source: Goskomstat of the Russian Federation.

Table 5. Urban CPI

(Monthly percentage change unless specified otherwise)

	Index Weight	Dec. 1990	Dec. 1991[1]	Jan. 1992	Feb. 1992	Mar. 1992	Apr. 1992	May 1992	June 1992	July 1992	Aug. 1992	Sep. 1992	Oct. 1992	Nov. 1992	Dec. 1992	Dec. 1992[2]
Food, beverages, and tobacco	0.5520	. . .	174.0	358.6	16.7	14.6	15.5	11.3	16.8	7.8	8.7	16.5	35.3	26.8	24.6	2,589.7
Beef	0.0226	. . .	488.2	345.1	3.8	4.6	1.6	11.8	6.7	8.1	8.5	16.5	37.3	30.3	22.6	1,654.3
Eggs	0.0113	. . .	243.6	265.3	−6.0	11.7	35.2	0.7	−5.6	4.0	8.7	31.3	68.8	20.1	31.4	1,848.8
Milk	0.0096	. . .	114.1	209.4	61.5	40.3	25.7	6.1	45.4	6.7	16.1	12.8	29.3	34.4	27.9	4,128.8
Butter	0.0310	. . .	249.7	912.7	14.5	4.2	14.5	5.1	2.6	−0.3	1.1	7.5	25.6	45.4	45.0	4,181.9
Vegetable oil	0.0081	. . .	153.2	234.9	27.3	49.5	28.7	16.6	4.8	1.6	6.0	13.3	48.5	39.3	41.2	3,473.9
Potatoes	0.0049	. . .	465.0	87.0	8.2	9.8	19.2	16.6	19.6	30.1	20.7	−9.8	2.0	31.9	24.9	779.0
Clothing and footwear	0.2297	. . .	223.6	187.2	40.4	21.1	15.8	3.4	2.6	3.1	5.6	11.1	18.2	23.2	19.5	1,163.4
Rent, water, fuel, and power	0.0208	. . .	35.0	272.1	40.6	9.1	8.5	13.8	17.9	14.5	4.6	9.5	11.5	17.1	10.3	1,468.7
Household goods	0.0626	. . .	163.2	295.8	60.7	22.7	21.7	6.0	4.7	4.0	9.2	10.8	26.6	25.5	30.9	2,663.8
Medicines	0.0037	. . .	6.2	410.0	10.6	19.6	30.4	25.5	13.7	13.5	18.8	7.7	16.6	10.3	52.1	3,461.3
Transport and communication	0.0461	. . .	−2.4	289.5	47.3	8.6	15.4	38.7	25.6	10.6	14.4	23.2	37.1	47.2	38.0	5,336.8
Recreation, education, and culture	0.0722	. . .	69.2	190.2	51.3	18.6	32.6	8.3	19.2	8.5	8.8	12.1	27.4	19.7	18.6	2,031.7
Personal care and effects	0.0129	. . .	162.5	178.5	39.1	30.1	25.1	4.4	5.7	2.5	4.6	10.2	14.4	18.8	34.4	1,399.8
Total, all items	1.0000	. . .	143.9	296.0	27.3	16.4	17.2	10.5	13.9	7.1	8.6	15.2	31.1	27.1	25.3	2,317.6

Source: Goskomstat of the Russian Federation.
[1] Percentage change from December 1990.
[2] Percentage change from December 1991.

Table 6. Consumer Price Inflation: International Comparison[1]

(Percentage change over previous period)

		Bulgaria[2]	Former Czechoslovakia	Poland	Romania[3]	Russia[4]
	1987	2.7	0.1	25.2	1.1	1.6
	1988	2.5	0.1	60.2	2.8	0.2
	1989	6.4	1.4	251.1	0.8	2.4
	1990	23.8	10.0	585.8	4.2	5.6
	1991	333.5	57.7	70.3	161.1	92.7
	1992	91.4	10.1	43.0	211.3	1,352.9
1989	January	. . .	. . .	11.0	. . .	. . .
	February	. . .	. . .	7.9	. . .	. . .
	March	. . .	. . .	8.1	. . .	. . .
	April	. . .	. . .	9.8	. . .	. . .
	May	. . .	. . .	7.2	. . .	. . .
	June	. . .	. . .	6.1	. . .	. . .
	July	. . .	. . .	9.5	. . .	. . .
	August	. . .	. . .	39.5	. . .	. . .
	September	. . .	. . .	34.3	. . .	. . .
	October	. . .	. . .	54.8	. . .	. . .
	November	. . .	. . .	22.4	. . .	. . .
	December	. . .	. . .	17.7	. . .	. . .
1990	January	1.9	. . .	79.6*	. . .	. . .
	February	1.8	. . .	23.8	. . .	. . .
	March	1.9	. . .	4.3	. . .	. . .
	April	1.9	. . .	7.5	. . .	. . .
	May	1.8	. . .	4.6	. . .	. . .
	June	4.1	. . .	3.4	. . .	. . .
	July	3.5	. . .	3.6	. . .	. . .
	August	10.9	. . .	1.8	. . .	. . .
	September	4.5	. . .	4.5	. . .	. . .
	October	4.1	. . .	5.7	. . .	. . .
	November	4.9	. . .	5.0	23.4*	. . .
	December	10.4	. . .	5.9	11.6	. . .
1991	January	13.6	25.8*	12.7	14.8	6.2
	February	122.9*	7.0	6.7	7.0	4.9
	March	50.5	4.7	4.5	6.6	6.3
	April	2.5	2.0	2.7	26.5*	52.2*
	May	0.8	1.9	2.7	5.1	2.5
	June	5.9	1.8	4.9	2.0	0.2
	July	8.4	−0.1	0.1	9.5*	−0.2
	August	7.5	—	0.6	11.2	0.1
	September	3.8	0.3	4.3	7.3	1.4
	October	3.3	—	3.2	10.4	4.2
	November	5.0	1.5	3.2	10.9	8.6
	December	4.9	1.1	3.1	13.7	12.0
1992	January	4.8	1.0	7.5	19.5	296.0*
	February	5.8	0.5	1.8	12.5	27.3
	March	3.9	0.3	2.0	10.0	16.4
	April	3.1	0.5	3.7	4.7	17.2
	May	11.9	0.4	4.0	12.1	10.5
	June	5.8	0.3	1.6	4.3	13.9
	July	2.8	0.9	1.4	3.2	7.1
	August	1.2	0.6	2.7	3.4	8.6
	September	3.4	1.8	5.3	10.1*	15.2
	October	6.2	2.0	3.0	9.6	31.1
	November	6.7	2.0	2.3	13.6	27.1
	December	4.6	0.8	2.2	13.2	25.3

Sources: IMF, *International Financial Statistics*; Bulgarian National Bank, *News Bulletin*; Goskomstat of the Russian Federation; and authors' estimates (for the yearly 1992 inflation rates).

[1] An asterisk denotes a month of major price reform or liberalization.

[2] For 1987–89, RPI; from 1990 onward, CPI.

[3] Through 1990, the annual data relate to a Paasche index of goods and services prices.

[4] State stores and consumer cooperatives index through 1989; consolidated RPI for 1990 and 1991; and urban CPI thereafter.

Table 7. Geographical Price Dispersion, December 1991–December 1992

(In rubles)

	In State Stores/City Markets											
	12/27	1/24	3/01	4/01	5/05	6/02	7/01	7/28	9/01	9/22	10/27	12/01
Beef (/kg)												
Moscow	20.6/100.0	36–87/130–225	92.0/139.8	64.4/225.0	58.9/248.6	57.4/244.2	66.1/266.1	77.8/282.4	84.4/343.4	92.0/402.1	123.8/512.9	176.4/651.4
St. Petersburg	37.5/118.0	79.7/225.0	50.0/121.4	51.5/125.0	88.0/180.0	86.9/172.0	85.9/243.0	87.7/251.0	88.9/243.0	91.5/360.0	105.3/400.0	204.0/550.0
Arkhangelsk (North)	45.0/60.0	65.1/70.0	72.5/. . .	72.5/. . .	82.1/120.0	80.6/120.0	83.5/NA	83.6/130.0	89.8/180.0	94.3/155.0	201.8/270.0	204.2/300.0
Saratov (Volga region)	17.0/40.0	50.0/45.0	. . ./. . .	. . ./. . .	NA/77.5	62.5/93.5	62.5/85.3	58.8/77.1	NA/100.0	98.0/130.0	125.7/157.5	143.6/191.2
Voronezh (Central Russia)	13.0/70.0	77.9/80.0	. . ./81.8	NA/90.0	NA/120.0	NA/110.0	73.5/90.0	73.5/86.3	NA/200.0	107.5/170.0	120.0/200.0	138.3/195.0
Krasnodar (South)	27.0/50.0	46.0/60.0	. . ./. . .	. . ./. . .	62.8/110.0	83.8/120.0	79.2/120.0	84.5/140.0	94.0/155.0	109.0/170.0	144.9/200.0	164.6/240.0
Yekaterinburg (Urals)	16.8/55.0	74.3/74.8	57.5/70.8	57.5/75.0	77.0/130.0	77.0/130.0	87.6/140.0	NA/160.0	93.5/190.0	91.2/190.0	150.6/250.0	215.5/290.0
Novosibirsk (Siberia)	23.2/60.0	55.0/75.0	83.1/75.0	NA/67.5	68.6/100.0	80.3/90.0	78.3/90.0	80.0/95.0	NA/150.0	95.6/150.0	118.8/180.0	156.6/230.0
Vladivostok (Far East)	. . ./. . .	. . ./. . .	. . ./. . .	. . ./. . .	80.4/142.5	95.6/157.5	NA/140.0	90.7/161.3	102.0/236.1	104.0/315.6	185.2/301.9	185.0/471.5
Eggs (/10 pieces)												
Moscow	9.7/20.0	16.0/NA	. . ./. . .	. . ./. . .	27.7/35.6	26.2/38.4	21.0/44.3	20.7/37.9	28.6/47.0	40.9/67.5	63.4/101.7	81.9/134.0
St. Petersburg	4.6/25.3	18.5/30.0	. . ./. . .	. . ./. . .	23.7/50.0	23.4/40.0	24.0/45.0	24.3/45.0	30.0/49.0	31.3/100.0	79.3/190.0	102.0/300.0
Arkhangelsk (North)	6.6/NA	13.6/NA	. . ./. . .	. . ./. . .	29.8/NA	26.9/NA	26.5/NA	24.5/NA	28.8/NA	36.6/NA	45.7/NA	68.6/NA
Saratov (Volga region)	7.0/11.0	15.0/14.7	. . ./. . .	. . ./. . .	18.0/NA	19.4/20.0	15.3/25.0	19.0/NA	28.0/NA	56.0/NA	60.0/60.0	57.4/75.0
Voronezh (Central Russia)	2.6/20.0	18.8/18.0	. . ./. . .	. . ./. . .	19.1/19.0	15.0/18.0	16.5/20.0	17.6/20.0	29.0/27.5	29.3/35.0	38.0/42.5	66.0/75.0
Krasnodar (South)	6.0/15.0	13.6/17.0	. . ./. . .	. . ./. . .	12.5/14.0	15.1/16.0	17.4/20.0	19.5/20.0	23.0/30.0	31.0/40.0	60.9/60.0	59.7/70.0
Yekaterinburg (Urals)	7.0/NA	NA/NA	. . ./. . .	. . ./. . .	26.8/NA	28.7/NA	24.3/NA	20.6/NA	18.9/NA	21.2/NA	43.6/NA	49.2/NA
Novosibirsk (Siberia)	6.5/15.0	15.3/20.0	. . ./. . .	. . ./. . .	30.5/25.0	23.4/25.0	21.2/20.0	23.0/25.0	25.7/30.0	35.0/NA	44.9/60.0	62.1/NA
Vladivostok (Far East)	. . ./. . .	. . ./. . .	. . ./. . .	. . ./. . .	20.0/NA	21.0/NA	35.0/40.0	34.0/35.9	40.0/NA	50.0/NA	110.0/NA	156.0/NA
Milk (/liter)												
Moscow	0.7/33.0	2.0/30.5	2.9/31.0	2.0/35.0	2.0/36.4	2.0/42.6	9.1/41.7	9.0/48.2	13.5/65.4	14.1/61.1	14.1/87.1	20.0/168.4
St. Petersburg	0.8/NA	1.6/25.0	9.0/. . .	NA/NA	8.6/NA	8.4/NA	9.5/NA	11.2/NA	11.5/NA	12.3/NA	20.9/70.0	29.5/150.0
Arkhangelsk (North)	NA/NA	3.1/NA	NA/. . .	NA/. . .	13.3/NA	20.0/NA	21.0/NA	15.7/NA	15.0/NA	19.1/NA	24.7/NA	30.2/NA
Saratov (Volga region)	1.2/4.0	1.3/6.1	. . ./. . .	. . ./. . .	4.5/NA	3.2/14.0	7.8/NA	7.8/11.0	7.8/20.0	7.8/20.0	12.0/34.0	16.0/50.0
Voronezh (Central Russia)	0.5/7.0	1.5/25.0	. . ./8.8	NA/10.0	1.3/8.3	2.9/7.5	4.0/10.8	4.0/10.8	5.0/13.5	5.0/13.3	8.0/20.0	10.0/31.5
Krasnodar (South)	1.6/6.0	1.6/10.0	. . ./. . .	. . ./. . .	1.6/17.0	7.9/16.0	7.9/16.0	11.3/18.0	16.8/20.0	19.1/33.0	24.1/33.0	33.8/40.0
Yekaterinburg (Urals)	4.5/10.0	1.8/5.9	5.0/16.0	4.8/20.0	5.4/NA	12.3/NA	12.7/20.0	13.7/NA	11.8/NA	14.7/NA	16.0/NA	16.0/100.0
Novosibirsk (Siberia)	0.5/NA	1.6/NA	6.9/NA	9.0/10.5	8.1/NA	7.6/13.0	8.4/NA	8.7/15.0	9.1/15.0	9.2/18.0	13.9/NA	22.5/NA
Vladivostok (Far East)	. . ./. . .	. . ./. . .	. . ./. . .	. . ./. . .	10.2/40.0	9.7/50.0	8.9/50.0	9.0/32.4	24.0/NA	26.8/35.0	35.7/102.9	39.3/145.6
Butter (/kg)												
Moscow	10.0/200.0	45–126.5/200.0	73.6/189.9	132.4/NA	147.1/300.0	186.5/200.0	188.3/241.4	185.0/253.1	187.6/286.0	201.2/428.1	264.2/487.3	415.4/819.3
St. Petersburg	8.6/100.0	49.6/275.0	163.5/167.7	157.0/275.0	189.0/300.0	182.2/NA	180.0/NA	183.7/NA	196.8/NA	232.4/NA	301.0/242.0	495.3/400.0
Arkhangelsk (North)	80.0/NA	171.6/NA	166.7/. . .	175.0/. . .	193.3/NA	194.2/NA	213.6/NA	180.6/NA	201.6/NA	202.4/NA	190.3/NA	328.7/NA
Saratov (Volga region)	24.0/60.0	121.8/105.6	. . ./. . .	. . ./. . .	175.6/NA	209.0/240.0	209.0/207.3	209.1/NA	206.2/230.0	203.4/232.0	232.0/300.0	358.3/400.0
Voronezh (Central Russia)	8.3/60.0	110.4/140.0	. . ./226.7	NA/170.0	164.4/175.0	156.7/140.0	155.6/160.0	160.6/150.0	170.0/NA	173.2/170.0	190.0/225.0	369.4/400.0
Krasnodar (South)	38.0/80.0	122.5/NA	. . ./. . .	. . ./. . .	193.5/200.0	196.4/200.0	196.7/200.0	187.1/200.0	199.9/230.0	227.0/250.0	313.2/350.0	447.4/450.0
Yekaterinburg (Urals)	NA/NA	201.0/NA	192.2/NA	198.0/280.0	183.7/NA	185.3/NA	194.0/240.0	183.0/NA	179.5/NA	199.6/NA	280.6/NA	381.6/NA
Novosibirsk (Siberia)	8.8/NA	198.7/150.0	196.4/168.5	165.0/150.0	159.1/160.0	159.7/150.0	166.1/155.0	171.0/170.0	179.9/NA	200.5/250.0	288.2/270.0	461.5/440.0
Vladivostok (Far East)	. . ./. . .	. . ./. . .	. . ./. . .	. . ./. . .	156.8/NA	154.2/NA	154.0/NA	185.0/NA	203.1/NA	203.6/NA	281.0/NA	. . ./NA

Vegetable oil (/liter)												
Moscow	35.0/50.0	16.3/50–100	20.8/80.0	27.0/80.0	34.8/80.3	40.8/85.1	37.3/123.1	38.4/125.3	47.9/143.2	59.2/169.5	86.0/180.0	149.6/295.0
St. Petersburg	2.6/63.8	17.1/82.0	10.6/99.0	19.0/NA	57.8/104.0	57.6/125.0	67.8/108.0	65.7/116.0	66.4/133.0	84.9/147.0	101.2/. . .	191.2/. . .
Arkhangelsk (North)	36.0/NA	17.0/NA	NA/. . .	NA/. . .	43.4/NA	39.9/NA	45.5/NA	50.6/NA	52.2/NA	62.5/NA	150.0/NA	220.0/NA
Saratov (Volga region)	3.0/11.0	15.7/18.7	. . ./. . .	. . ./. . .	20.3/NA	NA/NA	42.5/NA	NA/NA	55.0/NA	NA/NA	137.0/NA	157.7/NA
Voronezh (Central Russia)	3.0/24.0	9.0/20.0	. . ./27.3	NA/30.0	33.3/28.0	24.3/22.5	31.0/35.0	32.1/30.0	NA/NA	28.0/80.0	NA/100.0	NA/135.0
Krasnodar (South)	4.0/20.0	NA/20.0	. . ./. . .	. . ./. . .	20.6/35.0	33.0/42.0	34.3/35.0	36.0/40.0	40.0/45.0	56.0/70.0	92.9/90.0	115.0/110.0
Yekaterinburg (Urals)	2.7/NA	12.1/NA	NA/NA	30.0/80.0	49.5/NA	51.7/NA	51.4/100.0	53.0/100.0	54.1/100.0	64.2/110.0	92.3/NA	166.0/NA
Novosibirsk (Siberia)	2.9/NA	NA/80.0	. . ./NA	NA/80.0	77.5/80.0	73.8/80.0	71.7/75.0	65.2/80.0	68.1/NA	86.3/NA	172.0/NA	NA/290.0
Vladivostok (Far East)	. . ./. . .	. . ./. . .	. . ./. . .	. . ./. . .	NA/NA	77.5/NA	75.0/NA	75.0/70.0	68.8/NA	NA/NA	NA/NA	NA/NA
Potatoes (/kg)												
Moscow	3.2/25.0	4.8/15.0	4.2/15.1	4.6/10.6	7.7/10.6	7.2/23.0	6.8/38.8	11.4/39.3	20.9/31.1	23.6/32.4	22.1/30.7	30.2/55.6
St. Petersburg	3.4/8.5	7.0/13.0	8.0/15.0	7.8/15.0	11.4/15.0	9.0/11.0	7.9/13.0	13.4/35.0	26.0/31.1	24.3/28.0	25.6/. . .	45.1/. . .
Arkhangelsk (North)	3.0/3.0	2.8/4.8	9.0/. . .	5.2/. . .	6.3/8.0	7.4/8.0	6.4/8.0	NA/9.0	25.5/20.0	21.4/20.0	29.3/30.0	45.6/50.0
Saratov (Volga region)	3.0/5.0	3.1/7.8	. . ./. . .	. . ./. . .	7.0/8.0	6.0/8.6	6.0/10.0	23.0/27.3	NA/17.9	18.0/16.5	14.0/21.0	18.0/28.4
Voronezh (Central Russia)	2.0/7.0	5.0/9.0	NA/7.0	NA/7.5	4.3/7.0	7.2/7.0	5.9/NA	16.7/12.5	10.0/8.5	9.0/13.0	12.0/14.0	13.0/13.5
Krasnodar (South)	3.0/6.0	6.0/10.0	. . ./. . .	. . ./. . .	5.3/9.0	8.4/9.0	20.0/15.1	23.0/25.0	18.0/20.0	20.0/20.0	19.0/25.0	21.0/35.0
Yekaterinburg (Urals)	2.4/5.0	NA/NA	. . ./7.8	6.0/7.0	6.6/11.0	11.3/12.0	10.5/23.0	NA/50.0	26.0/25.0	25.8/25.0	23.2/25.0	32.7/35.0
Novosibirsk (Siberia)	2.0/NA	4.0/8.0	4.0/5.0	3.5/7.5	5.1/10.0	5.0/9.0	7.7/10.0	NA/30.0	13.0/18.0	15.2/15.0	14.7/20.0	23.5/35.0
Vladivostok (Far East)	. . ./. . .	. . ./. . .	. . ./. . .	. . ./. . .	9.0/12.3	9.0/12.7	13.9/37.8	14.0/29.6	28.4/25.5	35.0/30.6	34.1/26.8	31.9/50.2

Sources: Goskomstat of the Russian Federation; and Interfax, *Agriculture Report*, various issues.
Note: NA signifies that the item was not available.

Table 8: Ratio of City Market to State Store Prices for Selected Food Products, December 1991–December 1992

	12/27	1/24	3/01	4/01	5/05	6/02	7/01	7/28	9/01	9/22	10/27	12/01
						Beef						
Moscow	4.8	...	1.5	3.5	4.2	4.3	4.0	3.6	4.1	4.4	4.1	3.7
St. Petersburg	3.1	2.8	2.4	2.4	2.0	2.0	2.8	2.9	2.7	3.9	3.8	2.7
Arkhangelsk (North)	1.3	1.1	...	...	1.5	1.5	...	1.6	2.0	1.6	1.3	1.5
Saratov (Volga region)	2.4	0.9	...	...	...	1.5	1.4	1.3	...	1.3	1.3	1.3
Voronezh (Central Russia)	5.4	1.0	...	...	...	...	1.2	1.2	...	1.6	1.7	1.4
Krasnodar (South)	1.9	1.3	...	...	1.8	1.4	1.5	1.7	1.6	1.6	1.4	1.5
Yekaterinburg (Urals)	3.3	1.0	1.2	1.3	1.7	1.7	1.6	...	2.0	2.1	1.7	1.3
Novosibirsk (Siberia)	2.6	1.4	0.9	...	1.5	1.1	1.1	1.2	...	1.6	1.5	1.5
Vladivostok (Far East)	...	...	...	...	1.8	1.6	...	1.8	2.3	3.0	1.6	2.5
						Eggs						
Moscow	2.1	...	...	...	1.3	1.5	2.1	1.8	1.6	1.7	1.6	1.6
St. Petersburg	5.5	1.6	...	...	2.1	1.7	1.9	1.9	1.6	3.2	2.4	2.9
Arkhangelsk (North)	...	...	...	...	...	...	...	...	...	...	...	...
Saratov (Volga region)	1.6	1.0	...	...	...	1.0	1.6	...	...	...	1.0	1.3
Voronezh (Central Russia)	7.7	1.0	...	...	1.0	1.2	1.2	1.1	0.9	1.2	1.1	1.1
Krasnodar (South)	2.5	1.2	...	...	1.1	1.1	1.1	1.0	1.3	1.3	1.0	1.2
Yekaterinburg (Urals)	...	...	...	...	...	...	...	...	...	...	...	...
Novosibirsk (Siberia)	2.3	1.3	...	...	0.8	1.1	0.9	1.1	1.2	...	1.3	...
Vladivostok (Far East)	...	...	...	...	...	...	1.1	1.1	...	...	...	...
						Milk						
Moscow	50.8	15.6	10.8	17.5	18.2	21.3	4.6	5.4	4.8	4.3	6.2	8.4
St. Petersburg	...	16.0	...	...	...	...	...	...	...	...	3.3	5.1
Arkhangelsk (North)	...	...	...	...	...	...	...	...	...	...	...	...
Saratov (Volga region)	3.3	4.6	...	...	...	4.4	...	1.4	2.6	2.6	2.8	3.1
Voronezh (Central Russia)	15.2	16.7	...	...	6.4	2.6	2.7	2.7	2.7	2.7	2.5	3.2
Krasnodar (South)	3.8	6.4	...	...	10.6	2.0	2.0	1.6	1.2	1.7	1.4	1.2
Yekaterinburg (Urals)	2.2	3.4	3.2	4.2	...	...	1.6	...	...	...	...	6.3
Novosibirsk (Siberia)	...	...	...	1.2	...	1.7	...	1.7	1.6	2.0	...	...
Vladivostok (Far East)	...	...	...	...	3.9	5.2	5.6	3.6	...	1.3	2.9	3.7
						Butter						
Moscow	20.0	...	2.6	...	2.0	1.1	1.3	1.4	1.5	2.1	1.8	2.0
St. Petersburg	11.6	5.5	1.0	1.8	1.6	...	...	...	...	...	0.8	0.8
Arkhangelsk (North)	...	...	...	...	...	...	...	...	...	...	...	...
Saratov (Volga region)	2.5	0.9	...	...	...	1.1	1.0	...	1.1	1.1	1.3	1.1
Voronezh (Central Russia)	7.2	1.3	...	...	1.1	0.9	1.0	0.9	...	1.0	1.2	1.1
Krasnodar (South)	2.1	...	...	...	1.0	1.0	1.0	1.1	1.2	1.1	1.1	1.0
Yekaterinburg (Urals)	...	...	...	1.4	...	...	1.2	...	...	...	...	...
Novosibirsk (Siberia)	...	0.8	0.9	0.9	1.0	0.9	0.9	1.0	...	1.2	0.9	1.0
Vladivostok (Far East)	...	...	...	...	...	...	...	...	...	...	...	...
						Vegetable oil						
Moscow	1.4	...	3.9	3.0	2.3	2.1	3.3	3.3	3.0	2.9	2.1	2.0
St. Petersburg	24.2	4.8	9.4	...	1.8	2.2	1.6	1.8	2.0	1.7	0.0	0.0
Arkhangelsk (North)	...	...	...	...	...	...	...	...	...	...	...	...
Saratov (Volga region)	3.7	1.2	...	...	...	...	...	...	...	...	...	...
Voronezh (Central Russia)	8.0	2.2	...	...	0.8	0.9	1.1	0.9	...	2.9	...	...
Krasnodar (South)	5.0	...	...	...	1.7	1.3	1.0	1.1	1.1	1.3	1.0	1.0
Yekaterinburg (Urals)	...	...	...	2.7	...	...	1.9	1.9	1.8	1.7	...	...
Novosibirsk (Siberia)	...	...	...	...	1.0	1.1	1.0	1.2	...	...	...	...
Vladivostok (Far East)	...	...	...	...	...	...	...	0.9	...	...	...	...
						Potatoes						
Moscow	7.8	3.1	3.6	2.3	1.4	3.2	5.7	3.4	1.5	1.4	1.4	1.8
St. Petersburg	2.5	1.9	1.9	1.9	1.3	1.2	1.6	2.6	1.2	1.2	...	...
Arkhangelsk (North)	1.0	1.7	...	...	1.3	1.1	1.3	...	0.8	0.9	1.0	1.1
Saratov (Volga region)	1.7	2.5	...	...	1.1	1.4	1.7	1.2	...	0.9	1.5	1.6
Voronezh (Central Russia)	3.5	1.8	...	...	1.6	1.0	...	0.7	0.9	1.4	1.2	1.0
Krasnodar (South)	2.0	1.7	...	...	1.7	1.1	0.8	1.1	1.1	1.0	1.3	1.7
Yekaterinburg (Urals)	2.1	...	...	1.2	1.7	1.1	2.2	...	1.0	1.0	1.1	1.1
Novosibirsk (Siberia)	...	2.0	1.3	2.1	2.0	1.8	1.3	...	1.4	1.0	1.4	1.5
Vladivostok (Far East)	...	...	...	...	1.4	1.4	2.7	2.1	0.9	0.9	0.8	1.6

Sources: Goskomstat of the Russian Federation; and Interfax, *Agriculture Report*, various issues.

Table 9. Controls on Food Prices, Mid-1992
(In percent)

Product	Proportion of Cities in Which Price Remained Controlled[1]
Milk	44
Kefir	36
Fat cottage cheese	29
Rye bread	30
Mixed rye-wheat bread	28
Grade 1 and 2 wheat bread	32
Top-quality wheat bread	10
Sugar	30
Salt	17
Meat products	11
Butter	6
Vegetable oil	14

Source: Goskomstat of the Russian Federation.
[1] Sample of 132 cities.

Table 10. Availability of Selected Foodstuffs in State Stores in 1992[1]
(In percentage of number of cities)

	Item Available			
	Without lines	With lines	With coupons	Item Unavailable
Meat				
January	34.2	5.3	7.9	52.6
February	51.3	2.6	7.9	38.2
March	53.9	2.6	3.9	39.6
April	50.0	6.6	5.2	38.2
May	47.4	5.3	7.9	39.4
June	48.7	5.3	0.0	46.0
July	59.2	3.9	1.3	35.6
August	57.9	6.6	1.3	34.2
September	57.2	6.0	3.6	33.2
October	63.2	2.6	2.6	31.6
November	71.1	2.6	1.3	25.0
December	67.1	3.9	2.6	26.4
Milk products				
January	30.3	55.3	0.0	14.4
February	44.7	48.7	1.3	5.3
March	78.9	15.8	0.0	5.3
April	78.9	14.5	1.3	5.3
May	80.3	18.4	0.0	1.3
June	78.9	13.2	0.0	7.9
July	85.5	10.5	0.0	4.0
August	84.2	10.5	0.0	5.3
September	88.2	9.2	0.0	2.6
October	85.5	7.9	0.0	6.6
November	84.2	14.5	0.0	1.3
December	81.6	10.5	0.0	7.9
Butter				
January	39.5	9.2	13.2	38.1
February	75.0	14.5	2.6	7.9
March	78.9	1.3	10.5	9.3
April	90.8	0.0	7.8	1.3
May	92.1	0.0	3.9	4.0
June	92.1	2.6	1.3	4.0
July	97.4	0.0	2.6	0.0
August	97.4	0.0	1.3	1.3
September	78.9	2.6	2.6	15.9
October	86.8	1.3	2.6	9.3
November	77.6	3.9	2.6	15.9
December	60.5	3.9	6.6	29.0
Vegetable oil				
January	1.3	9.2	19.7	69.8
February	11.8	2.6	21.1	64.5
March	21.1	2.6	21.1	55.2
April	36.8	0.0	11.8	51.4
May	56.6	1.3	14.5	27.6
June	51.3	0.0	5.3	43.4
July	52.6	0.0	9.2	38.2
August	56.6	2.6	5.3	35.5
September	40.8	2.6	2.6	54.0
October	42.1	1.3	2.6	54.0
November	47.4	2.6	3.9	46.1
December	51.3	1.3	2.6	44.8
Sugar				
January	1.3	11.8	32.9	54.0
February	5.3	3.9	40.8	50.0
March	14.5	1.3	26.3	57.9
April	19.7	3.9	30.3	46.1
May	40.8	2.6	26.3	30.3
June	43.4	1.3	23.7	31.6
July	50.0	2.6	21.1	26.3
August	51.3	1.3	22.4	25.0
September	34.2	5.3	17.1	43.4
October	36.8	3.9	19.7	39.6
November	53.9	2.6	19.7	23.8
December	55.3	0.0	15.8	28.9
Bread				
January	22.4	28.9	17.1	31.6
February	65.8	28.9	3.9	1.4
March	81.6	18.4	0.0	0.0
April	80.3	17.1	0.0	2.6
May	82.9	14.5	0.0	2.6
June	77.6	2.6	11.8	8.0
July	85.5	11.3	0.0	3.7
August	84.2	10.5	0.0	5.3
September	84.2	13.2	1.3	1.3
October	86.8	11.8	0.0	1.4
November	85.5	9.2	0.0	5.3
December	84.2	10.5	0.0	5.3

Table 10 ***(concluded)***

	Item Available: Without lines	Item Available: With lines	Item Available: With coupons	Item Unavailable
Eggs				
January	67.1	2.6	7.9	22.4
February	88.2	0.0	9.2	2.6
March	75.0	6.6	3.9	14.5
April	90.8	2.6	1.3	5.3
May	93.4	2.6	1.3	2.7
June	93.4	3.9	0.0	2.7
July	97.4	1.3	1.3	0.0
August	96.1	2.6	1.3	0.0
September	90.8	1.3	2.6	5.3
October	89.5	1.3	0.0	9.2
November	90.8	2.6	1.3	5.3
December	80.3	1.3	2.6	15.8

	Item Available: Without lines	Item Available: With lines	Item Available: With coupons	Item Unavailable
Potatoes				
January	63.2	3.9	0.0	32.9
February	90.8	1.3	0.0	7.9
March	81.6	0.0	0.0	18.4
April	71.1	1.3	0.0	27.6
May	77.6	0.0	0.0	22.4
June	65.8	0.0	0.0	34.2
July	39.5	0.0	0.0	60.5
August	67.1	0.0	0.0	32.9
September	90.8	0.0	0.0	9.2
October	89.5	1.3	0.0	9.2
November	89.5	1.3	0.0	9.2
December	86.8	0.0	0.0	13.2
Vegetables				
January	76.3	1.3	0.0	22.4
February	88.2	1.3	0.0	10.5
March	88.2	0.0	0.0	11.8
April	86.8	0.0	0.0	13.2
May	90.8	0.0	0.0	9.2
June	86.8	1.3	0.0	11.9
July	86.8	0.0	0.0	13.2
August	93.4	0.0	0.0	6.6
September	93.4	0.0	0.0	6.6
October	96.1	1.3	0.0	2.6
November	90.8	1.3	0.0	7.9
December	90.8	0.0	0.0	9.2

Source: Goskomstat of the Russian Federation.
[1] Availability at the end of the month in a sample of 76 major cities.

Table 11. Household Income, Expenditure, and Saving

	1991												1992											
	J	F	M	A	M	J	J	A	S	O	N	D	J	F	M	A	M	J	J	A	S	O	N	D
	(In billions of rubles)																							
Income	33.7	38.7	42.5	45.0	45.1	52.6	77.8	65.3	67.4	78.2	83.7	125.2	119.6	175.3	226.4	349.9	272.3	370.3	509.0	536.6	624.1	754.7	907.1	1,467.2
Taxes and duties	4.5	4.5	4.5	4.6	4.6	3.9	4.5	5.2	5.3	7.4	8.3	10.4	11.2	16.0	25.6	25.3	29.4	41.4	48.1	58.6	75.9	83.7	89.9	141.2
Disposable income	29.2	34.2	37.9	40.4	40.6	48.7	73.3	60.1	62.1	70.8	75.4	114.9	108.4	159.3	200.9	324.6	242.9	328.9	460.8	478.0	548.2	671.0	817.2	1,326.0
Expenditure on goods and services[1]	25.3	26.0	32.1	32.3	35.5	36.7	41.3	43.8	46.2	52.8	56.4	77.7	82.3	122.6	153.5	178.9	190.5	217.2	258.8	304.8	385.6	468.7	558.3	851.0
Accumulation of deposits and securities	5.0	5.7	2.9	4.4	2.4	2.1	20.7	4.2	5.8	10.5	7.4	17.5	10.8	14.3	8.5	78.7	10.1	19.3	19.9	17.5	24.2	27.2	38.2	169.8
Accumulation of cash	−1.2	2.3	2.8	3.6	2.8	9.8	11.1	12.0	9.8	7.5	11.3	19.4	16.8	22.5	38.9	67.9	42.1	91.4	182.1	155.7	138.4	175.1	220.7	305.2
Total saving[2]	3.7	8.0	5.7	8.0	5.2	11.9	31.8	16.2	15.6	17.9	18.7	36.9	27.7	36.7	47.4	146.6	52.2	110.7	202.0	173.3	162.6	202.3	258.9	475.0
	(In percent)																							
Saving rate with respect to:																								
Gross income	11.1	20.8	13.4	17.9	11.6	22.6	40.9	24.8	23.2	22.9	22.4	29.5	23.1	21.0	20.9	41.9	19.2	29.9	39.7	32.3	26.1	26.8	28.5	32.4
After-tax income	12.8	23.6	15.0	19.9	12.9	24.5	43.4	26.9	25.2	25.3	24.9	32.2	25.5	23.1	23.6	45.2	21.5	33.6	43.8	36.2	29.7	30.1	31.7	35.8
Share of saving as:																								
Cash	−33	29	49	45	54	82	35	74	63	42	60	53	61	61	82	46	81	83	90	90	85	87	85	64
Noncash	133	71	51	55	46	18	65	26	37	58	40	47	39	39	18	54	19	17	10	10	15	13	15	36

Source: Goskomstat of the Russian Federation.

Note: The 1991 data exclude the frozen part of the April 1991 deposit compensation (rub 71.9 billion). However, the compensation paid on bonds is included in the April 1991 figures, and the compensation on demand deposits that could be withdrawn starting in July 1991 (rub 18.2 billion) is included in the July 1991 figures. The rub 71.9 billion were unfrozen in April 1992 and have been added to income and to saving for that month.

[1]Including VAT.

[2]Excludes saving in the form of insurance policies.

Table 12. Overdue Cash Payments to Individuals

(In billions of rubles, beginning of month)

	1992									1993
	April	May	June	July	August	September	October	November	December	January
Total	31.8	78.5	149.9	221.6	114.0	. . .	. . .	. . .	. . .	. . .
Of which:										
Delayed wage payments in industry, agriculture, and construction	14.6	22.2	54.4	65.1	47.6	28.2	21.5	29.9	33.6	28.8
of which:										
industry	9.0	14.9	35.7	44.5	30.5	17.3	11.6	20.1	17.7	15.1
agriculture	2.0	2.3	5.4	9.1	8.9	4.5	3.6	4.4	6.6	5.8
construction	3.4	5.0	13.4	11.6	8.2	6.4	6.4	5.4	9.3	7.9
of which:										
owing to shortage of cash in banks	9.6	13.1	38.4	46.4	28.7	7.9	2.8	2.5	1.3	0.6
Overdue social allowance and wage payments in sectors other than industry, agriculture, and construction	17.2	56.3	95.5	156.5	66.4	. . .	. . .	. . .	. . .	. . .
Owing to shortage of cash in banks (for all payments)	26.7	69.4	134.0	202.9	. . .	. . .	. . .	. . .	. . .	. . .

Source: Goskomstat of the Russian Federation.

Table 13. Wage Structure Across Sectors
(In rubles per month and ratio to overall average)

	1991					1992				
Sector	I	II	III	IV	Year	I	II	III	IV[1]	Year[1]
National average	318	426	554	910	552	2,056	3,986	6,327	12,139	6,127
Industry	340	447	596	1,033	604	2,612	4,763	7,042	13,671	7,022
	1.07	1.05	1.08	1.14	1.09	1.27	1.19	1.11	1.13	1.15
Agriculture	259	302	440	931	484	1,092	2,260	4,361	9,579	4,323
	0.81	0.71	0.79	1.02	0.88	0.53	0.57	0.69	0.79	0.71
Forestry	227	303	397	665	398	1,519	2,707	5,158	9,268	4,663
	0.71	0.71	0.72	0.73	0.72	0.74	0.68	0.82	0.76	0.76
Transport	364	508	678	1,070	655	2,804	6,048	9,082	17,314	8,812
	1.14	1.19	1.22	1.18	1.19	1.36	1.52	1.44	1.43	1.44
Communications	276	428	522	770	499	1,709	3,211	6,120	11,224	5,566
	0.87	1.00	0.94	0.85	0.90	0.83	0.81	0.97	0.92	0.91
Construction	401	539	759	1,081	695	2,773	5,197	8,947	16,127	8,261
	1.26	1.27	1.37	1.19	1.26	1.35	1.30	1.41	1.33	1.35
Trade, public catering, material-technical supplies, and other	271	347	462	804	471	1,544	3,184	5,490	10,622	5,210
	0.85	0.81	0.83	0.88	0.85	0.75	0.80	0.87	0.88	0.85
Information processing services	323	438	502	781	511	1,717	3,229	5,629	10,457	5,258
	1.02	1.03	0.91	0.86	0.93	0.84	0.81	0.89	0.86	0.86
Housing, communal services, nonproductive household services	249	356	460	699	441	1,746	3,216	5,484	9,666	5,028
	0.78	0.84	0.83	0.77	0.80	0.85	0.81	0.87	0.80	0.82
Health care, physical training, social security	240	382	424	618	416	1,210	2,692	4,399	7,295	3,899
	0.75	0.90	0.77	0.68	0.75	0.59	0.68	0.70	0.60	0.64
Public education	256	373	366	561	389	1,259	2,931	3,586	7,060	3,709
	0.81	0.88	0.66	0.62	0.70	0.61	0.74	0.57	0.58	0.61
Culture[2]	222	327	316	547	353					
	0.70	0.77	0.57	0.60	0.64					
						1,111	1,752	3,680	5,657	3,050
						0.54	0.44	0.58	0.47	0.50
Arts[2]	279	381	409	647	429					
	0.88	0.89	0.74	0.71	0.78					
Science and science services	387	455	551	667	515	1,518	2,900	4,798	8,888	4,526
	1.22	1.07	0.99	0.73	0.93	0.74	0.73	0.76	0.73	0.74
Finance and state insurance	475	727	905	1,837	986	2,613	5,475	10,629	26,927	11,411
	1.49	1.71	1.63	2.02	1.79	1.27	1.37	1.68	2.22	1.86
Government employees, public organizations staff, etc.	362	440	522	836	540	1,739	3,423	6,085	11,289	5,634
	1.14	1.03	0.94	0.92	0.98	0.85	0.86	0.96	0.93	0.92
Memorandum item:										
Minimum wage	80	120	140	180	130	342	528	900	900	668
	0.25	0.28	0.25	0.20	0.24	0.17	0.13	0.14	0.07	0.11

Source: Goskomstat of the Russian Federation.
[1]Preliminary.
[2]For 1992, the culture and arts categories are combined.

Table 14. Distribution of Population by Income Level

(Monthly incomes per capita)

Income Bracket *(In rubles)*	Proportion in Bracket *(In percent)* 1990	1991	1992 I	1992 II	1992 August	1992 November
0–100	11.4	0.3				
101–150	27.2	3.1				
151–200	26.0	8.3	0.1			
201–250	17.2	12.5				
251–300	9.6	14.0	0.1	0.5	0.3	
301–350	5.1	13.3	0.4			
351–400	2.6	11.4	0.7			
401–450	0.3	9.2	1.2			0.5
451–500	0.2	7.1	1.7			
501–600	0.1	9.5	5.1			
601–700		5.2	7.1			
701–800		2.8	8.6	7.1	4.7	
801–900		1.5	9.3			
901–1,000		0.8	9.4			
1,001–1,100			9.0			
1,101–1,200			8.3			
1,201–1,300			7.4	14.7	11.6	2.5
1,301–1,400			6.5			
1,401–1,500			5.7			
1,501–1,600			4.8			
1,601–1,700			4.0			
1,701–1,800			3.4	16.7	14.9	5.0
1,801–1,900			2.8			
1,901–2,000			2.4			
2,001–2,500				15.1	14.8	7.2
2,501–3,000				12.4	13.0	8.4
3,001–3,500	0.1	1.0		9.7	10.8	8.9
3,501–4,000				7.4	8.7	8.8
4,001–4,500				5.6	6.9	8.4
4,501–5,000				4.2	5.4	7.7
5,001–5,500				3.2	4.2	7.0
5,501–6,000			2.0	2.4	3.3	6.2
6,001–6,500						5.5
6,501–7,000						4.8
7,001–7,500						4.2
7,501–8,000						3.6
8,001–8,500				1.0	1.4	3.2
8,501–9,000						2.7
9,001–9,500						2.4
9,501–10,000						2.1
over 10,000						0.9
Total	100.0	100.0	100.0	100.0	100.0	100.0

Source: Goskomstat of the Russian Federation.

Table 15. Household Savings

(Ruble cash and deposits)

Period		Nominal Household Balances (End-period, in billions of rubles) [3]	Nominal Household Balances [4]	Real Household Balances (1987=100)[1] [3]	Real Household Balances [4]	Per Capita Wage Equivalent (In months)[2] [3]	Per Capita Wage Equivalent [4]
1987		196.7		100.0		6.0	
1988		219.9		110.9		6.1	
1989		253.1		122.9		6.2	
1990		301.5		136.2		6.3	
1991	January	305.2		137.8		6.8	
	February	313.2		134.1		6.6	
	March	318.9		129.0		6.3	
	April	326.9		86.4		5.6	
	May	332.1		85.8		5.2	
	June	344.0		88.0		5.0	
	July	375.8	447.7	93.6	102.1	5.4	5.9
	August	392.0	463.9	99.9	118.6	4.7	5.6
	September	407.6	479.5	102.4	120.8	4.1	4.9
	October	425.5	497.4	102.8	120.6	3.7	4.3
	November	444.2	516.1	98.7	115.1	3.4	4.0
	December	481.1	553.0	93.5	108.1	2.8	3.3
1992	January	508.8	580.7	25.3	29.0	2.3	2.7
	February	545.5	617.4	21.1	24.0	1.8	2.0
	March	592.9	664.8	19.6	22.1	1.4	1.6
	April	739.5		19.5	20.6	0.7	0.7
	May	791.7		20.4		1.4	
	June	902.4		19.7		1.1	
	July	1,104.4		21.8		1.2	
	August	1,277.7		23.9		1.4	
	September	1,440.3		23.6		1.2	
	October	1,642.6		20.4		1.2	
	November	1,901.5		18.5		1.1	
	December	2,376.5		17.7		0.9	

Sources: Goskomstat of the Russian Federation; and authors' calculations.

[1]Real indices computed using estimated period averages.

[2]Ratio of per capita savings to national average wage in period ended. For 1991, quarterly wage data were interpolated to construct a notional monthly series.

[3]Including the unfreezing of rub 71.9 billion of deposits in April 1992 as an addition to household balances in that month.

[4]Including the rub 71.9 billion that remained frozen until April 1992 as an addition to household balances in July 1991.

References

Barr, Nicholas, *Income Transfers and the Social Safety Net in Russia*, Studies of Economies in Transformation, Paper No. 4 (Washington: World Bank, 1992).

Bruno, Michael, "Stabilization and Reform in Eastern Europe: A Preliminary Evaluation," *Staff Papers*, International Monetary Fund, Vol. 39 (December 1992), pp. 741–77.

Center of Economic Analysis and Forecasting, *Russia—1993: Economic Situation*, Issue 1 (Moscow, February 1993).

Gimpelson, Vladimir, "Changing Work Attitudes in Russia's New Private Sector," *RFE/RL Research Report*, Vol. 2 (February 5, 1993), pp. 37–40.

Goskomstat, *Economic Results of the Russian Federation in 1991* (Moscow, 1992).

Institute of Economic Policies, *Russian Economy in the Fall of 1992: Trends and Prospects* (Moscow, December 1992).

International Energy Agency, *Energy Prices and Taxes: Fourth Quarter 1992* (Paris: Organization for Economic Cooperation and Development, 1993).

International Monetary Fund and others, *A Study of the Soviet Economy*, 3 vols. (Paris, 1991).

International Monetary Fund, *Russian Federation: Economic Review* (Washington, April 1992).

———, *Russian Federation: IMF Economic Reviews*, No. 8 (Washington, forthcoming 1993).

Koen, Vincent, and Steven Phillips, "Price Liberalization in Russia: The Early Record," IMF Working Paper 92/92 (Washington: International Monetary Fund, November 1992).

Organization for Economic Cooperation and Development, *Short-Term Economic Statistics: Central and Eastern Europe* (Paris, 1992).

Osband, Kent, "Index Number Biases During Price Liberalization," *Staff Papers*, International Monetary Fund, Vol. 39 (June 1992), pp. 287–309.

Popkin, Barry M., Marina Mozhina, and Alexander K. Baturin, "The Development of a Subsistence Income Level in the Russian Federation" (unpublished; University of North Carolina at Chapel Hill, December 8, 1992).

Roberts, Bryan W., "The J-Curve Is a Gamma-Curve: Initial Welfare Consequences of Price Liberalization in Eastern Europe" (unpublished; Massachusetts Institute of Technology, July 1992).

Weitzman, Martin L., "Price Distortion and Shortage Deformation or What Happened to the Soap?" *American Economic Review*, Vol. 81 (June 1991), pp. 401–414.

Recent Occasional Papers of the International Monetary Fund

104. Price Liberalization in Russia: Behavior of Prices, Household Incomes, and Consumption During the First Year, by Vincent Koen and Steven Phillips. 1993.

103. Liberalization of the Capital Account: Experiences and Issues, by Donald J. Mathieson and Liliana Rojas-Suárez. 1993.

102. Financial Sector Reforms and Exchange Arrangements in Eastern Europe. Part I: Financial Markets and Intermediation, by Guillermo A. Calvo and Manmohan S. Kumar. Part II: Exchange Arrangements of Previously Centrally Planned Economies, by Eduardo Borensztein and Paul R. Masson. 1993.

101. Spain: Converging with the European Community, by Michel Galy, Gonzalo Pastor, and Thierry Pujol. 1993.

100. The Gambia: Economic Adjustment in a Small Open Economy, by Michael T. Hadjimichael, Thomas Rumbaugh, and Eric Verreydt. 1992.

99. Mexico: The Strategy to Achieve Sustained Economic Growth, edited by Claudio Loser and Eliot Kalter. 1992.

98. Albania: From Isolation Toward Reform, by Mario I. Blejer, Mauro Mecagni, Ratna Sahay, Richard Hides, Barry Johnston, Piroska Nagy, and Roy Pepper. 1992.

97. Rules and Discretion in International Economic Policy, by Manuel Guitián. 1992.

96. Policy Issues in the Evolving International Monetary System, by Morris Goldstein, Peter Isard, Paul R. Masson, and Mark P. Taylor. 1992.

95. The Fiscal Dimensions of Adjustment in Low-Income Countries, by Karim Nashashibi, Sanjeev Gupta, Claire Liuksila, Henri Lorie, and Walter Mahler. 1992.

94. Tax Harmonization in the European Community: Policy Issues and Analysis, edited by George Kopits. 1992.

93. Regional Trade Arrangements, by Augusto de la Torre and Margaret R. Kelly. 1992.

92. Stabilization and Structural Reform in the Czech and Slovak Federal Republic: First Stage, by Bijan B. Aghevli, Eduardo Borensztein, and Tessa van der Willigen. 1992.

91. Economic Policies for a New South Africa, edited by Desmond Lachman and Kenneth Bercuson with a staff team comprising Daudi Ballali, Robert Corker, Charalambos Christofides, and James Wein. 1992.

90. The Internationalization of Currencies: An Appraisal of the Japanese Yen, by George S. Tavlas and Yuzuru Ozeki. 1992.

89. The Romanian Economic Reform Program, by Dimitri G. Demekas and Mohsin S. Khan. 1991.

88. Value-Added Tax: Administrative and Policy Issues, edited by Alan A. Tait. 1991.

87. Financial Assistance from Arab Countries and Arab Regional Institutions, by Pierre van den Boogaerde. 1991.

86. Ghana: Adjustment and Growth, 1983–91, by Ishan Kapur, Michael T. Hadjimichael, Paul Hilbers, Jerald Schiff, and Philippe Szymczak. 1991.

85. Thailand: Adjusting to Success—Current Policy Issues, by David Robinson, Yangho Byeon, and Ranjit Teja with Wanda Tseng. 1991.

84. Financial Liberalization, Money Demand, and Monetary Policy in Asian Countries, by Wanda Tseng and Robert Corker. 1991.

83. Economic Reform in Hungary Since 1968, by Anthony R. Boote and Janos Somogyi. 1991.

82. Characteristics of a Successful Exchange Rate System, by Jacob A. Frenkel, Morris Goldstein, and Paul R. Masson. 1991.

81. Currency Convertibility and the Transformation of Centrally Planned Economies, by Joshua E. Greene and Peter Isard. 1991.

80. Domestic Public Debt of Externally Indebted Countries, by Pablo E. Guidotti and Manmohan S. Kumar. 1991.
79. The Mongolian People's Republic: Toward a Market Economy, by Elizabeth Milne, John Leimone, Franek Rozwadowski, and Padej Sukachevin. 1991.
78. Exchange Rate Policy in Developing Countries: Some Analytical Issues, by Bijan B. Aghevli, Mohsin S. Khan, and Peter J. Montiel. 1991.
77. Determinants and Systemic Consequences of International Capital Flows, by Morris Goldstein, Donald J. Mathieson, David Folkerts-Landau, Timothy Lane, J. Saúl Lizondo, and Liliana Rojas-Suárez. 1991.
76. China: Economic Reform and Macroeconomic Management, by Mario Blejer, David Burton, Steven Dunaway, and Gyorgy Szapary. 1991.
75. German Unification: Economic Issues, edited by Leslie Lipschitz and Donogh McDonald. 1990.
74. The Impact of the European Community's Internal Market on the EFTA, by Richard K. Abrams, Peter K. Cornelius, Per L. Hedfors, and Gunnar Tersman. 1990.
73. The European Monetary System: Developments and Perspectives, by Horst Ungerer, Jouko J. Hauvonen, Augusto Lopez-Claros, and Thomas Mayer. 1990.
72. The Czech and Slovak Federal Republic: An Economy in Transition, by Jim Prust and an IMF Staff Team. 1990.
71. MULTIMOD Mark II: A Revised and Extended Model, by Paul Masson, Steven Symansky, and Guy Meredith. 1990.
70. The Conduct of Monetary Policy in the Major Industrial Countries: Instruments and Operating Procedures, by Dallas S. Batten, Michael P. Blackwell, In-Su Kim, Simon E. Nocera, and Yuzuru Ozeki. 1990.
69. International Comparisons of Government Expenditure Revisited: The Developing Countries, 1975–86, by Peter S. Heller and Jack Diamond. 1990.
68. Debt Reduction and Economic Activity, by Michael P. Dooley, David Folkerts-Landau, Richard D. Haas, Steven A. Symansky, and Ralph W. Tryon. 1990.
67. The Role of National Saving in the World Economy: Recent Trends and Prospects, by Bijan B. Aghevli, James M. Boughton, Peter J. Montiel, Delano Villanueva, and Geoffrey Woglom. 1990.
66. The European Monetary System in the Context of the Integration of European Financial Markets, by David Folkerts-Landau and Donald J. Mathieson. 1989.
65. Managing Financial Risks in Indebted Developing Countries, by Donald J. Mathieson, David Folkerts-Landau, Timothy Lane, and Iqbal Zaidi. 1989.
64. The Federal Republic of Germany: Adjustment in a Surplus Country, by Leslie Lipschitz, Jeroen Kremers, Thomas Mayer, and Donogh McDonald. 1989.
63. Issues and Developments in International Trade Policy, by Margaret Kelly, Naheed Kirmani, Miranda Xafa, Clemens Boonekamp, and Peter Winglee. 1988.
62. The Common Agricultural Policy of the European Community: Principles and Consequences, by Julius Rosenblatt, Thomas Mayer, Kasper Bartholdy, Dimitrios Demekas, Sanjeev Gupta, and Leslie Lipschitz. 1988.
61. Policy Coordination in the European Monetary System. Part I: The European Monetary System: A Balance Between Rules and Discretion, by Manuel Guitián. Part II: Monetary Coordination Within the European Monetary System: Is There a Rule? by Massimo Russo and Giuseppe Tullio. 1988.
60. Policies for Developing Forward Foreign Exchange Markets, by Peter J. Quirk, Graham Hacche, Viktor Schoofs, and Lothar Weniger. 1988.
59. Measurement of Fiscal Impact: Methodological Issues, edited by Mario I. Blejer and Ke-Young Chu. 1988.

Note: For information on the title and availability of Occasional Papers not listed, please consult the IMF *Publications Catalog* or contact IMF Publication Services.